HEART ATTACK
At Red Rock Canyon

ENDLESS DREAMS
The BulletBall Guy

COPYRIGHT

Title Book: HEART ATTACK At Red Rock Canyon
Author Book: Marc K. Griffin

2020, Marc K. Griffin
Bulletball55@gmail.com

9781716649028

DEDICATED TO:

* My sister Janet Marie Griffin rest in heaven big sis
* My wife Alline Walker-Griffin for loving me as I am
* My daughter Kristin Walker for accepting me as I am
* My bro Anthony Davis, Sr. for keeping me focused

* A Higher Power
* Everyone else whose path I crossed on the road to infinity
* The music that plays in my head and lives in my soul
* Dr. Branavan Umakanthan, DO for saving my life

TABLE OF CONTENTS

PROLOGUE — 6

GUNSIGHT NOTCH — 9

BEAUTY — 25

FIVE SECONDS — 42

OH SHIT — 60

LOVE — 86

ADVENTURE — 108

PAIN — 132

SADNESS — 155

HAPPINESS — 173

PEACE — 187

EPILOGUE — 199

HEART ATTACK

PROLOGUE

"I could be well moved if I were as you. If I could pray to move, prayers would move me. But I am as constant as the northern star, of whose true fixed and resting quality. There is no fellow in the firmament. The skies are painted with unnumbered sparks. They are all fire and every one doth shine. But there's but one in all doth hold his place. So in the world. 'Tis furnished well with men. And men are flesh and blood and apprehensive. Yet in the number I do know but one. That unassailable holds on his rank. Unshaked of motion. And that I am 'he'."

As a freshman in high school when I first read these words spoken by Julius Caesar my heart changed. There was nothing life could throw at me that I would not and could not defeat because I was 'he'.

Now 50 years later I underwent another change of heart in my never ending search for internal peace.

GUNSIGHT NOTCH

Just 30 minutes earlier I was marveling within myself at how good my body was responding to this difficult hike in Red Rock Canyon. I felt strong, blessed, and confident that I was on track to conquer Gunsight Notch. But within a matter of seconds I had transitioned from unwavering confidence to complete despair.

It was clear that something was deathly wrong. The dull pain I was withstanding in the center of my chest seemed unusual. I had to take shorter and slower breaths to lessen its ache. It felt like congestion from a chest cold. Except I didn't have a chest cold.

I stood frozen in time clutching the handle of my trekking pole to steady myself on the mountain's edge. I could no longer entice my body to continue climbing.

The sounds of nature that surrounded me faded away and all I could hear was the relentless pounding of my heart, beating against the sternum, trying to unearth more oxygen out of the higher altitude. I closed my eyes and consciously attempted to catch my breath again.

But my breath could not be caught.

My body waned.

While trying to make sense of this gravity I became confused. Fatigue was a normal experience when climbing to a mountain top. Total exhaustion, on the other hand, was not. As of two minutes ago there was nothing normal about this adventure. I could not wrap my head around what was happening inside my mind, my body, or my soul to cause this aberration.

My nerves began to fray as the dilemma I faced became more and more alarming.

Literally and figuratively standing at the precipice of Gunsight Notch I needed to remain composed and think my way out of this unbalance of myself. One breath and one step at a time.

Beginning with my elevated blood pressure, I needed to cool my body down. So I unzipped my Timberland hiking jacket, allowing the breeze to cool my torso. Even with the cooler morning temperature I noticed that my shirt was drenched with sweat. Fuck, that meant I was probably dehydrated.

I could feel the dryness in my throat and wondered why I hadn't noticed it before now.

Suddenly I felt thirsty and needed water from my backpack. My brain was moving a mile a minute as it reached for the backpack strap but my arm remained frozen. It would not give my brain the authority to control its movement. There was obviously something more immediate than dehydration going on within my system. The water would have to wait.

I felt this moment was an impasse. Believing in the mind over matter theory, I was taken aback that matter had weakened the mind enough to finally reign triumphant. So I decided to hush my fear and listen to my inner being. This allowed me to pick up on other more subtle clues that my physical functions were experiencing a major shutdown. For the first time in my hiking life it felt as if the wilderness had beaten me. I questioned if I would even be able to convince myself to continue beyond this point.

Taking further stock of my predicament, I looked up towards the col and realized that even taking a single step towards the summit was problematic.

On the other hand, the descent would improve my oxygen intake. So I quickly turned my attention to the valley floor from whence I came. The journey down the mountain appeared futile as well. In my mind's eye, what should appear to be a simple two mile hike back to civilization looked like an eternity. My energy was totally spent so I leaned heavily on the trekking pole to help me relax and conserve as much energy as possible.

Once again my body waned and I felt my knees buckle.

Exhaustion was the only answer. I was barely able to stop myself from flat-out falling on my face by forcing more weight onto the trekking pole to hold myself upright.

Next to me was a boulder the height of a chair. So I decided to sit, rest, and gather myself.

Sitting on the rock did nothing to slow my breathing or relieve the pain inside my chest. Resting my head in the palm of my hand I could not understand why my body was experiencing a total breakdown.

I became seized by fear again. My mind quickly grabbed hold of the panic looming inside me as I recovered my equanimity.

Options? I needed options. The one thing I did know was that staying in the wilderness was not an option. I had to make a decision. I needed to make a decision and take that first step. So I chose to head back down the mountain as quickly as possible. Actually it was my only logical choice.

An unwritten rule when mountain climbing is that once you have reached the halfway point to your destination there is no turning back. I had just scrambled halfway up the mountain when this disaster struck. To stop and retreat is one of the most difficult decisions one can make once traveling beyond that imaginary point of no return.

GUNSIGHT NOTCH WILDERNESS TRAIL

In this Red Rock Canyon wilderness, I found myself alone and secluded on a trail less traveled. Uncertain which was worse, the pain I felt inside my body or the disappointment of not being able to continue climbing.

When hiking, even during the most harrowing of moments, I had never lost complete confidence in my climbing prowess.

Over the past half century I had learned to read my body in combination with the surrounding environment to determine whether or not conditions were suitable to reach the summit.

Occasionally, in my thirst for an adventure I would underestimate the degree of difficulty in reaching the peak causing a trek of precarious challenges. Particularly when hiking in unfamiliar territory because it can slow your progress and time awareness is extremely important when hiking. Trying to descend in the darkness can make for an unfortunate misadventure. But whatever the tribulations of the past I never lost my self-confidence about the outcome. I was the consummate optimist when faced with perilous circumstances.

However, on this day, January 26, 2020, fear had

trumped self-assurance. My ability to continue traversing the mountain's path towards Gunsight Notch was no longer in question. I wasn't even certain that I could make it back to the trailhead.

My backpack made me feel constricted but I was too drained to unshouldered it. Pushing up with the assistance of my trekking pole, I forced myself to stand. This sudden motion caused my blood pressure to drop which resulted in light headedness. Pushing through the dizziness I turned to begin the descent. Another mistake.

My mind could no longer control its matter and balance finally gave way to gravity. I fell backward onto the boulder. The backpack prevented my head from hitting the oversized rock. In controlled slow motion I utilized the trekking pole to slide down the boulder and land safely on the narrow sandy dirt path below. Resting against the rock, I instinctively unbuckled the backpack to loosen its hold on my chest and slipped it off my shoulders. I closed my eyes to shut out the external world, allowing my mind to focus on slowing down the breathing.

'In and out, in and out, in and out'.

Maintaining my cadence of breathing, my mind drifted into a song by Delerium, *"Give me release ... Give me peace ... Comfort me I can't hold it all in ... Heaven holds a sense of wonder and I want to believe ... in this white wave I am sinking in this silence I believe ... I have seen you ... you are breathing...".*

I looked up at the clouds in the sky and spoke aloud, "If you want to make God laugh, tell him your plans." But it was not his laughter I heard. It was mine. Without question, God had chosen a different kind of journey for me this day. I could only guess that it was a lesson in humility because right now I felt extremely humbled.

I sat on the wilderness floor with a single minded focus on continuing to control my breathing.
'In and out, in and out, in and out'.

In the distant recess of my thoughts I could hear nature's music beginning to reemerge. I could hear leaves rustling in the breeze, the scampering of chipmunks, and the chirping of birds. I also heard the echoes of mountaineers somewhere in the distance. They were shouting back and forth while scaling a sheer rock face. A natural communication process for the teamwork required between rock climbers.

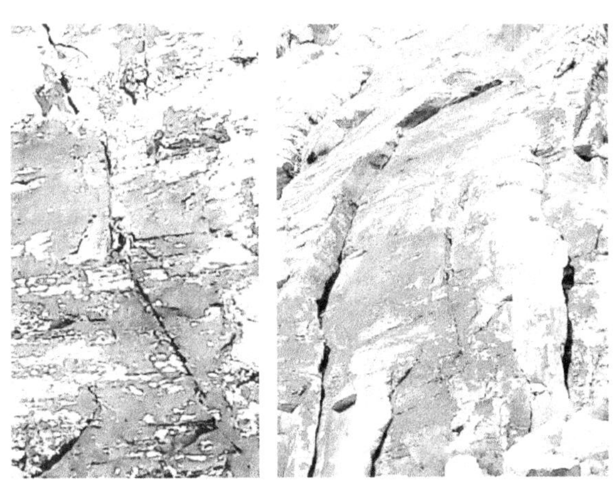

PINE CREEK CANYON ROCK FACE

I was too weak to give a shout out for assistance. The battle taking place inside me took every ounce of vigor. I couldn't even give thought as to the reason why death was seeking me out. I was just instinctively trying to bring my mind, body, and soul back into alignment.

Once again I would have to face the greatest fear in my life ... running out of lives. They say a cat has nine lives. This was only my sixth in almost 65 years. Surely I was still due at least three more do-overs. At least.

It was a feeling that I had experienced five other times before and had obviously survived.

But this moment somehow felt different. More aged. Like how I imagined an undefeated heavyweight boxing champion would feel when looking up from the canvas for the first time.

I opened my eyes and looked up from my canvas ...

Seeing God's horizon I couldn't help but smile as the feeling of calm poured over me. The desert, mountains, clouds, and sun all came together and created bliss ... transposing into the music of Bliss, *"Now I drift to you The stars high above Part of the sky Like the air that I breathe You'll always be there The wings that I need When I wanna fly ...".*

It was an exceptionally beautiful Sunday morning. The unbridled joy of viewing God's creation even during the most dire of circumstances was an incredibly soothing feeling and a wonderful gift.

This was a moment that required a video to commemorate the occasion. My mind instinctively reached into the jacket pocket for the cell phone but my arm remained unresponsive. Total weakness had engulfed my body once again.

So my mind decided to remain absolutely quiet, allowing for my animal instincts to take command as the means for survival. The ability to turn over control of my inner being to my instincts only occurred when death was imminent. The natural inclination for holding on to life can circumvent both the mind and body. Creating a separate and indistinct level of uncompromising die-hardism.

My arm then reached and unzipped the backpack for water. So I just sat and quenched my thirst. Allowing the guzzled water to flow freely down my chin. Slowing only when a breath or two was required.

Regaining just enough energy, I reached into my jacket pocket and found the cellphone ... as anticipated there was no reception. Not that I would have ever used it to call for help. Pride before the fall.

HORIZON FROM GUNSIGHT NOTCH TRAIL

Refusing to allow this moment to be lost forever, I used my cellphone to capture the stunning view and the complete ambiance of this time. 'HEAVEN MUST BE LIKE THIS' would be my final expression on this earth as I recorded the morning horizon. It brought tears to my eyes, a smile of contentment to my face, and serenity to my heart.

This was my time to find out the answer to creation and I simply could not think of a better way to leave this world. For my heavenly journey God has blessed me with a majestic view of nature's valley. A view that would be shared with the world once my physical self was discovered by others.

Feeling at peace I just sat and allowed my spirit to soak in the fate of my good fortune as Blank and Jones filled my mind, *"Close your eyes and lean back. You are here ... Relax. Slow down. Feel yourself drifting, Like floating on a cloud ... Cherish the moment ... here and now. Relax. Slow down ...".*

My eyes began to close and the vivid colors of Gunsight Notch that surrounded me began to dissipate. And once again the sounds of nature began to fade.

My past life started to flash in front of my eyes. These flashes and nature's beauty before me began to collide, switching back and forth, one trying to dominate the other. It is true that years of retrospect can flow through you in a matter of seconds when death approaches.

My virtues of love, pain, sadness, happiness, beauty, adventure, and peace were on full display. All the people that I loved, all the pain that I caused, all the sadness I have felt, all the happiness that I shared, all the beauty that I've seen, all the adventures I've experienced, and the peace that I feel at this very moment ... all of it came and went in the bat of an eye.

And out here in the mountains, where life and death are equal partners, was my perfect self fulfilling prophecy. It is where I feel most alive and where death always looms close by. And though my end was near I did not fear its coming. In complete tranquility my mind floated towards the gates of heaven ... it was an alluring vision.

It's beauty reminded me of my wife as the words of Maxwell floated into my hypnotic state, *"All the things we should have said that I never said. All the things we should have done that I never did. All the things we should have given but I didn't ...".*

As my head slowly rolled back to lay softly on nature's canvas I could see the majesty of Gunsight Notch Peak just beyond my reach.

And I thought to myself *'Goodbye Milky Way'* as Enigma spoke, *"Mission is over. Mission is done. I will miss you children of the sun. But it's time to go away. I go home until someday. I say goodbye, goodbye Milky way."*

As Gunsight Notch faded into darkness my endless dreams were finally coming to an end. Yea, though I walk through the shadow of the valley of death I will fear no evil ...

In the supine position my eyes closed.

SHADOW OF THE VALLEY OF DEATH

All of nature's beauty that existed in my heart flashed before my eyes as I remembered each addictive moment experienced in the wilderness.

My mind drifted ...

In 1983, 10 years after graduating high school, I found my true calling in life as I stood inside an old lookout atop Harney Peak in the Black Hills of South Dakota.

HARNEY PEAK

I watched in awe as high winds brought a thunderous

storm across the darkened sky straight towards me. My mind screamed for me to take cover but my body remained frozen. And for the first time in my life the 'mind over matter' theory simply did not apply. Animal instincts did.

Unable to shake loose the fear in my heart, yet somehow maintaining the courage to stand in defiance, the low flying cumulonimbus clouds of the approaching tempest washed over me. I continued to hold my ground as the crack of thunder filled the air and flashes of lightning surrounded me. And though I felt the impact of roaring winds and the sting of frozen pellets I gave no quarter. I stilled myself by breathing in the moment.

'In and out, in and out, in and out'.

It all seemed surreal. It seemed a dream. Except it wasn't. It was magical.

Never a believer of coincidence, I knew that I was at this very peak at this very moment on purpose. Soaked of rain I was blessed with God's baptism as the storm *continued to pass through on its way to bless others in its wake.*

As the skys cleared in the distance the faint colors of a rainbow began to grow more vivid and glowed across the horizon.

I was afraid to blink in fear of missing a detail. And I didn't.

It was the sudden appearance of a second rainbow, bigger and bolder than the first, that swept away any doubt that a higher power existed. And though God had not yet spoken to my heart, the exhilaration I felt spoke volumes. He had gifted me with a change of heart ...

MOUNT MOOSILAUKE

Back in 1992 the trail leading up to Mount Moosilauke followed along side a beautiful cascade. It was my very first trek in the White Mountains of New Hampshire and I was overwhelmed. The music of nature was hypnotic as it flowed in unison with the lilting notes of water crashing onto the steep rocks as it rushed past. And as if on beat the forest swayed as the wind captured each leaf on every tree. A variety of birds seemed to sing together in harmony and my ears rejoiced in their music. The earth tones of the forest were so vivid that they made my body quiver in the pit of the stomach.

My eyes were hypnotized as they continually moved back and forth soaking in the wilderness candy that surrounded them. But always staying alert in search of any anomaly. The White Mountains are known for its wildlife. Black bear, moose, and bobcat was high on my list of concerns. The forest was thick with trees and shrubbery which allowed the animals to roam in anonymity. The unmistakable scent of fresh dung permeated through my nose as it penetrated the natural smell of the forest.

I could hear the buzzing and feel the brush of insects against my skin acknowledging their own presence in this wilderness. It was exhilarating to have all my senses at work simultaneously. And in that moment I was one with nature.

The trail would occassionally crisscross the cascade making for a challenging climb. The clear fresh water that glided over the stones would lure you to relax in its propinquity. To complete my mind's eye I half expected to see salmon swimming up stream. I didn't discover that the stream was deeper than it looked and the stones more slippery than imagined until it was too late.

As I crossed the cascade's camouflaged hazzards the unsuspected deep and rushing undercurrent caused me to loose my balance. The slick stones gave way as I attempted to right myself. Dropping my hiking stick, I reached up in a desperate attempt to grab hold of overhanging branches to prevent a disaster. It felt like slow motion as I missed the branches and lost my footing. I splashed into the water and landed on my ass. Quickly getting to my feet to minimize the soaking of my clothes I couldn't help but laugh at myself, just before realizing my hands were empty.

I could see my hiking stick sliding down the cascade and tumble over the chute. So I made a mental note to search for it on my descent.

During my spill, the forest had fallen completely quiet as if time was standing still. After finally making my way across the stream, as if on cue, the entire life of the wilderness re-emerged in concert. The forest as the birds sang, the wind blew, the trees *ruffled, the water rushed, insects flew, the sunlight flickered, and the unique smells in the woods filled my nostrils. Everything completely as it was before I fell. I experienced a full-bodied adrenalin rush of joy, fear, levity, and alertness all rolled up into one magical gist. This was my first experience with such an amazing phenomenon and I was moved some kind of way.*

At its core the wilderness is a place of immeasurable beauty. Not only in appreciation of its bearing but also its reciprocity. All the entities of indigenous life interdependent in its survival to exist. I was honored to be remotely considered a part of the clique. Clearly there was a powerful force within the forest that had captured my heart.

As I laid on the Red Rock mountain's floor my breathing slowed. I could feel my life continuing to fade away. I thought of a million ways to find the face of beauty as Vargo whispered in my mind, *"Find the face of beauty. So much to hear, to feel, to see. Each moment's a discovery. A million ways to find the face of beauty. To find the face of beauty ... the beauty of nature is very fragile ...".*

My flashback continued ...

Even though drenched from the slippage I was determined to continued hiking to the summit of Moosilauke. A light drizzle began to fall under the canopy of conifers and its pitter-patter joined in on the symphony of nature's music. An occasional cone would dislodge from the trees and hit the ground like the timbre of tambourines in an orchestra.

The coolness of the wind-blown rain gave me chills. I had not prepared my backpack with the necessary gear for rain so I would have to continue without a plastic poncho to wear.

When I broke the treeline it was apparent that the sunlit sky had dissolved into low lying fast moving dark clouds. They were crammed over the mountain's peak when at the crack of thunder the drizzle burst into a deluge.

Without the cover of trees I felt like a sitting duck without feathers to protect him from the elements. The wind blew and the rain poured. I embraced the moment by looking up at the heavens and thanking God for such a beautiful experience. Like a born optimist I had turned the mountain into a goldmine.

When I reached the peak the temperature dropped and the cooling wind turned into coldness. The deep gray clouds of the noreaster almost appeared to be within arms length of my reach. In awe of God's indefatigable creation I walked over to the brow of the peak, looked in the face of the most nefarious cloud of the tempest and threw my hands up in victory. All the storm clouds, their thunder, and their rain continued rushing across the wide summit.

Beyond the vista of the noreaster and all its fury followed the brilliance of sunshine. A remider that no *matter the power of life's storm, God is almighty.*

I kept my arms stretched towards the sky and at the top of my lungs screamed to the heavens until the darkness of the firmament gave way to the luminous glow of the sun.

The Godsend experience made clear in my heart once again the existence of infinity and life everlasting. I believe that this moment absolutely could not have been happenstance. It was created to bring a necessary spiritual fulfillment missing from my heart. It made me a more fitted man.

In the blink of another flashback I had driven across the Canadian border to the U.S. and spent the night on Mackinac Island ...

The hotel room had a jacuzzi with a view so I spent the evening relaxing and watching the large drifting flakes of a winter snow storm. Getting an early start I hopped in the Saab on my way home to Southfield

Michigan. The Upper Peninsula was thick with forest so I decided to find a place to park and investigate the surroundings. Snow mobile tracks caught my attention so I impromptu pulled into the next snow mobile trail and parked. A learned experience from my father's random sense of adventure. Collecting my backpack and trekking pole it was time to hike. The forest was eerily quiet as I trekked a wildlife pathway that disappeared into a mist of snowflakes. The environment was just right for an encounter.

Life continued to drain from my body that laid on a Gunsight Notch Trail and I could feel myself starting to slump forward as another 10th of a second slipped pass. Life was disappearing inchmeal yet memories flowed in lightspeed. They moved together and separate at the same time.

Life and death were both 'Here With Me' as I heard the voice of Dido, *"I wonder how I am still here. And I don't want to move a thing. It might change my memory ... And I won't go. I won't sleep. And I can't breathe ... And I won't leave."*

Just ahead I saw heaven's gate as my slow float continued ...

On full alert in the unknown wilderness of the Upper Peninsula I sensed the danger before I actually saw the threat. Standing perfectly still to mute the sound of crunching snow I scanned the snowy forest looking for anything out of the ordinary. Blinking my eyes to clear the snow away I saw two unusual figures stepping out onto the trail. As I honed in on the gray objects I noticed the yellowish color of eyes staring back. Four piercing eyes of two adult size wolves less than 50 yards away. As our eyes locked my immediate thought was to wondered if they were hungry.

My second thought was on the gun I had forgotten under the carseat.

Having read about such encounters I understood the

importance of not running away or turning my back. Also wolves are intelligent animals and wary of humans. So I stood taller and prominently displayed my trekking pole so as not to exhibit fear. Then according to the rules of encounter I began to slowly back away, never loosing eye contact.

The adrenalin mixture of excitement and fear was compelling. I could feel the pounding of my heart against my chest as I soaked in the dangerously beautiful moment. It felt good.

After a few seconds of hesitation, as if silently communicating, the wolves suddenly bolted across the path and disappeared into the woods.

Uncertain as to their whereabouts this was my cue to disappear as well. To save time I decided to cut through the forest. As I ran back towards the car I could hear rustling sounds not far behind that caused me acute stress.

Instinctively all I could think was fight-or-flight.

Taking a peek back I saw flashes of yellow

approximately 25 yards away. The decision of flight took hold causing me to flounder my way through the dense forest. Once the car came into view I began pressing the faab to unlock the door. Grabbing the handle I blundered my way into the car. Once inside, while laughing hysterically, I flipped on the wipers to clear the fallen snowflakes from the window and no more than 10 yards away I could see one set of piercing eyes staring from the trail. As I looked at the woods from which I had just crossed the other set of yellow eyes were unmistakable. Their divide and conquer tactic almost worked. Almost.

I could feel my heart pumping the adrenalin through my veins and it was euphoric. One day I would come back to revisit this neck of the woods...

Another 10th of a second passed and my chin rested in the neck of my collar bone as I continued to fade into darkness ...

Hiroshima sang and reminded me to have faith, "Save

yourself for me. Nothing can go wrong. There will be another day. Look ahead so unafraid. Faith in love is all you need. Tell me once that you believe...".

I could feel my lips mouth the words, "I believe." Hiroshima continued, "Save yourself for me. 'Til the end of time ... the end of time ... end of time."

As I listened to the words of Hiroshima, at the exact same moment but in a separate space of my mind's eye, I was standing on top of Mount Lafayette in 1993. It was the most perfect day imaginable and the most beautiful view to behold. From its perch I could see the entire range of White Mountains.

... Then standing on the peak of Mount Katahdin in 1993. It was the most perfect day imaginable and the most beautiful view to behold.

... Then in 1986 I was standing in the middle of the Badlands of South Dakota. It was the most perfect day imaginable and the most beautiful view to behold.

... Standing at the point of Cape Flattery. It was the

most perfect day imaginable and the most beautiful view to behold.

... Standing under Niagara Falls. It was the most perfect day imaginable and the most beautiful view to behold.

... Swimming at midnight in the Hawaiian Islands. It was the most perfect day imaginable and the most beautiful view to behold.

... Hiking in the wilderness of Mount Rainier. It was the most perfect day imaginable and the most beautiful views to behold.

... Sitting with Alline on the Bluffs Of Castlewood overlooking the Meremec River. It was the most perfect day imaginable and the most beautiful view to behold.

... Standing atop Turtlehead Peak in Red Rock. It was the most perfect day imaginable and the most beautiful view to behold.

... Standing above Acolodona Falls with Kristin and Alline. It was the most perfect day imaginable and the most beautiful view to behold.

The closer my flashbacks got to present-day the sight in my mind's eye grew dimmer. The lack of oxygen was causing my body to completely shut down as my goodbyes were coming to an end. It was time to finally say farewell to my beautiful wife as my mind flashed pass our wedding vows ...

As I laid on the mountain's floor at peace with my

spiritual journey to God's house I was struck by the words my wife spoke this morning and every morning I go hiking, "Come back home to me."
I could feel the tears of cessation rolling down my cheeks and for the first time in this wilderness I spoke to God, "Please give me the strength ...".

But he was already taking my breath away.

TURTLEHEAD PEAK

I decided to complete the four mile hike up to Turtlehead Peak for the fifth time since moving to Las Vegas. This time to my dismay the dizziness struck early and often. I hadn't climbed very far so it was totally unexpected. I decided that the lack of consistency in my hiking life was causing my body to underperform. I needed to start hiking more often to retrain my body and improve its stamina.

I hadn't yet reached the point of no return so I sat along the cliff edge to partake in the trail mix and water from my backpack while enjoying the valley view of Red Rock Canyon. After an hour of relaxation I apologized to God and terminated the climb. Our deepest conversations were usually had on a mountain top. It would have to wait.

VIEW FROM TURTLEHEAD PEAK

Out of concern about dizziness during my last few hiking experiences I decided to visit my primary physician for a checkup. I had the usual near high blood pressure, Graves Disease, and high cholesterol. My bloodwork did not show any cause for serious concern.

Three weeks later I attempted Turtlehead Peak once again. This time I climbed slowly and deliberately to the peak. I pushed past the anxiety, fatigue, and slight dizziness that I felt. Reaching the summit raised my level of confidence and reinforced the feeling that there were no physical concerns. It gave me a false sense of invincibility.

I decided to step up my game and select a more challenging mountain to climb. Though I was unfamiliar with Gunsight Notch, based on the reviews I read it seemed a good choice. It had a steep ascent to the top that required strong scrambling skills and a keen eye for bearings. Both abilities that happen to match my strengths.

PINE CREEK TRAILHEAD TO GUNSIGHT NOTCH

Two months ago was my first attempt at reaching the peak of Gunsight Notch. It was another four mile climb to the summit but with a higher degree of difficulty compared to Turtlehead Peak. I had gotten a rather late start so I had to hike with a sense of urgency to reach the mountain top before noon.

During the hike fatigue struck early-on and I was unable to regain my stamina. I knew it was impossible to muster up enough energy to complete the journey on schedule so I aborted before reaching the halfway point of the climb. Disappointed, I vowed to be better prepared on my next attempt at scaling the Notch.

Today, January 26, 2020, would be that day.

Partly cloudy, zero humidity, and a high of 71 degrees. The perfect day for a hike. This time around I got an early start, felt better physically, and had a high confidence level. When climbing, your mental disposition is as important as the physical readiness.

I had planned a day trip to Red Rock Canyon to climb Gunsight Notch. My alarm buzzed at 5 a.m. It was time to rise, shine, and make a cup of hazelnut coffee in preparation for a great day.

The night before my journey I would organize my Outdoor backpack starting with my Winchester 38 revolver, all-purpose stainless steel knife, first aid kit, Nike Fit Dry fingerless gloves, 3 water bottles, snacks, fruit, and Precision Made binoculars. Then I would review the AllTrails AP map one last time and entrust the details to memory.

JANUARY 26, 2020

In the morning Alline, like she always did, kissed me goodbye and gave me a long look of concern as a reminder to stay safe.

Before every trip to the mountains she would always say, "I wish you wouldn't go but I know there's no stopping you. Come back home to me. I love you."

Slipping on my Stetson hiking hat while walking out the door I responded as I have forever, "Bye bye baby. I love you more." The expression of our love is built around 'always' and 'forevers'.

Shortly thereafter I hopped into my Lexus SUV, hooked up the bluetooth to Pandora, and switched to the Vargo Radio Station. It was my go-to music before a major hike. Its chill-out ambient sound set the right mood for a challenging climb. I always began with my favorite song, 'Wake Up' by Melibea.

To insure a successful trek I also stopped at the local convenience store and bought an extra bottled water and a bag of trail mix. I took a photo of the extra supplies and texted it to Alline. I knew that it would put her more at ease. I was not going to have a sustenance problem today. But we both knew that no matter how much I prepared, when in the wilderness expect the unexpected.

As I opened the sunroof, the words of Thievery Corporation filled the air, *"I feel alright, alright I feel strong, I feel rigid ... Oh feels so right, so right ... Happy ... 'Til the sunlight burns you happy, 'Til the sunlight burns a happy hole in Your heart, In your heart, In your heart."*

I arrived at Red Rock Canyon State Park at 6:15 a.m. and entered using my National Parks Senior Lifetime Admission Card. After a relaxing and scenic 15 minute sunrise drive thru the park I arrived at my destination: The Pine Creek Trail Entrance.

It was time to begin my journey. So to step up the mood I played the 'We Will Rock You' song by Queen. Over the years, as a general manager, it was a song I played over the intercom every morning to assemble and motivate the team prior to opening. Every associate in the building would immediately stop their task and start clapping to the beat as they made their way toward the front door entrance. We all begin our work day with the right attitude.

I danced to the reverberating beat as the music filled the mountainous air,*"Buddy you're a boy make a big noise playing in the streets gonna be a big man someday. We will we will rock you."*

I changed into my Timberland low cut hiking shoes, strapped on my backpack, and put on my fingerless gloves. Every detail meticulously completed as the beat continued, *"Gonna take on the world someday ... We will we will rock you. Sing it. We will we will rock you."*

Slipping back on my Stetson hiking hat and Chine sunglasses, I scanned the mountainside until locating the actual notch on the peak of Gunsight Notch. There are no trail signs or direct pathways to the summit for this particular climb. It was an intentional effort by the park service to discourage the novice hiker from attempting such a daunting climb to the peak.

I stored the mountain view and surrounding sky in my memory bank just in case I failed to identify the subtle man made markers along the way.

After my mental prehike gameplan, I grabbed my trekking pole and headed down a trail in the direction of Gunsight Notch.

GUNSIGHT NOTCH TRAIL

Even for an experienced climber, this was an exceptionally difficult trek. By far, the best way to determine the correct path was to identify obscure cairns that led up the mountain wilderness toward the Notch. On the way, there were two valleys to cross that were doable but tough to traverse.

Given the degree of difficulty, all in all, I felt very confident that the peak was well within reach this time.

I felt easy. Easy like Sunday morning. Then I realized

that Lionel Richie played in my head, *"I want to be high, so high, I wanna be free to know the things I do are right, I want to be free. Just me. I'm easy like Sunday morning."*

And I smiled. It was the perfect Sunday morning for a climb up high, so high. To be free. Just me.

After an uneventful first hour of hiking I let my guard down and was startled by a bird nesting nearby causing me to almost jumping out of my skin. It snapped me back from my daydreaming state.

Based upon the eye test I appeared to have completed about half the distance to the summit. This was apparent because of the change in landscape. As the tree line began to disappear there was a dramatic increase in elevation.

From this point the hike up to the col will require more scrambling because of the huge boulders and steep incline.

This was also considered the point of no return. My adrenalin began to flow from the excitement of the moment. The most dangerous section of the climb was approaching and all my senses were on high alert.

I could see the col approximately 1/2 mile further up the mountain. Once reaching the col its incline to the peak was not as steep and the way up becomes more defined. I imagined the view would be incredibly beautiful as the notch came within reach. My exhilaration in anticipation for the adventure yet to come caused my adrenalin to spike once again.

I felt short winded and the pressure of a cold

developing in my chest. I immediately started to feel anxious because it was not the first time in recent hikes that this feeling emerged. I assumed that my body was probably adjusting to the lack of oxygen in the higher altitudes.

Imagine my surprise when minutes later this normal feeling of fatigue turned into full blown exhaustion. My body was so weakened that I couldn't take another step.

I searched my memory with over 30 years of mountain climbing experience for an answer and none existed.

Something wasn't right. I felt confused. Uncertain. In the past I had dealt with issues of fatigue, not enough sustenance, or the lack of oxygen but the ideal of physically breakingdown seemed foreign. It never occurred to me that there were some things completely out of my control. Not meaning in the mountain wilderness but out of my control internally.

Even though I was well over 60 years of age and moved

more slowly and deliberate when hiking, God hadn't convinced me of my mortality until now.

I knew first hand the risks involved with trekking alone in the wilderness. When descending into desert canyons there are poisonous snakes, unforgiving cactus, and carnivorous animals. The challenges when ascending mountains involved slippery rocks, the dangers of scrambling up boulders, and falling off the edge of cliffs.

Almost all of the wilderness trails I traversed and mountain peaks I climbed were classified as 'difficult' and this required experienced hikers, which severely limited potential hiking doggs.

Anyway, the solitude when hiking trails and climbing mountains had become the perfect natural environment to communicate with my God.

The interactions between us was private. This required hiking without companions.

We shared dialogue on love, pain, sadness, happiness,

adventure, beauty, and peace. It was our conversation on these topics that touched my soul and gave me faith to believe in his existence.

I enjoyed the heartfelt talks as we struggled to continue building our relationship. God had a wonderful way of guiding our back and forth bantering towards the purposeful intent of creating a more thoughtful examination of 'life after death'.

The necessity for these conversations was extremely important to me because without them I felt incomplete. Or maybe the more accurate word is faithless.

God knows that as long as I continue to struggle up every mountain in search of him, it meant that my faith in him was strong.

So even though the challenge of reaching a mountain's peak was full of unexpected danger it was completely worth the risk. I feared what would happen inside my soul if I was no longer able to reach the summit where God and I always talked.

These were the most important encounters of my life.

Spending quality time with God gifted me with the joy of bringing home an extraordinarily celestial spirit.

These thoughts, past adventures, and other significant moments up until this very moment were racing through my mind within five seconds after I had closed my eyes to usher in my spiritual journey …

My final memories continued to flash before my eyes as I floated toward God's gate.

Then through the words of Enigma I heard God's voice, *"The experience of survival. Try to think about it. That's the chance to live your life and discover. Try to think about it. The experience of survival ...".*

VIVID MOUNTAIN WILDERNESS

And just before life faded into pitch-black darkness my brain suddenly exploded. It felt like an electric shock had released a million needles into its nucleus creating an intense tingling sensation throughout my body. The vivid colors of the mountain's wilderness accompanied the explosion as if bursting out of a black hole. Leading me back to my wedding day vows.

Simultaneously with this discharge of energy came a remembered revelation that made me shout out loud, "OH SHIT!"

While at death's door my diminishing thoughts recalled a promise made on July 24, 2014 ... five years ago. I had guaranteed Alline at least ten wonderful years of marriage and this was only year number five! I absolutely could not leave this earth yet because I knew that my wife would be thoroughly pissed if I didn't live up to my end of the deal. To my promise. To my guarantee.

This abrupt awakening of my soul transported me from my serene ascension to the heavens back to my draconian reality in the Gunsight Notch wilderness.

I attempted to open my eyes. I hadn't noticed my eyes were already opened from the remembered proclamation I had spoken to my wife.

As I focused my gaze up at the sky, floating into view before my eyes was the face of beauty looking at me. Alline's alluring stare was fused within the clouds, reminding me of my promise. Giving me purpose to survive.

ALLINE WALKER GRIFFIN

The power of our love had stood fast at death's door. My heart filled with affection as Roberta Flack played in my head, *"The first time ever I saw your face I thought the sun rose in your eyes And the moon and the stars Were the gifts you gave ... I felt your heart so close to mine And I knew our joy would fill the earth And last til the end of time ...".*

I had been blessed with a miracle and my premonition of death had exited stage left. The pain in my chest subsided just enough to give me strength for a new beginning.
God gifted me with a change of heart.

The possibility of surviving the day came to the forefront of thought as a resolute rush of positive energy flooded my being. I flashed back to the last time I had felt such conviction for survival. The time when I risked everything on BulletBall. When on national television I disagreed with all four judges and said, "It was meant to be. BulletBall will be a success and that I guarantee." Having lived through that humiliating moment and all the syndicated shows that followed meant I could survive anything. And I had.

It was time to direct all my newfound confidence into the current dilemma at hand. In order to escape the wilderness I would have to get down from this mountain and traverse through the valley.

But first, I have to get on my feet. I knew that just trying to stand was going to be a difficult task but I was not in control anymore. The power of Alline's love is what receded the attack on my heart and brought back my spirit.

I gripped the trekking pole for support. Steadying myself, I rose from the ground while grabbing the backpack and slinging it over my right shoulder.

It was an over ambitious move. My equilibrium faltered so I quickly unshouldered the backpack and used it as a counter- balance to the trekking pole.

Remaining calm and keeping my head down to prevent another bout with postural hypotension, my eyes remained fixed on the pathway immediately around my brown Timberland low cut hiking shoes.

Standing completely still was all I could do not to collapse again. I immediately sat on the boulder next to me and began to consciously rhythm my breathing.

'In and out, in and out, in and out'.

I sensed my lungs regaining control of their oxygen intake. My rapid heartbeat slowly subsided to a manageable level and I could feel my body gaining enough strength to begin the journey home.

Before getting started, I needed to drink water to prevent dehydration. I set the backpack on the boulder next to me, unzipped it, and removed a plastic bottle of water. Still exhausted, it took three attempts before I could garner enough strength to twist off the cap and take a drink. When I poured some of the water over my head to cool off was when I realized that my Stetson was missing. I felt the gnome of Murphy's Law.

PRIZE HAT

It was the hiker's hat that Alline gifted me for my birthday. I could never leave this place without it. Scanning the mountainside I saw the hat about twenty yards down the cliff edge. Smirking while shaking my head in disbelief I was once again reminded of Murphy's Law. God was not making this adventure easy and I could ill afford to make any more mistakes.

If I went down to retrieved the hat there was no way I would be able to climb back up. I looked for an alternate route and just right of the hat was a brim that would allow me to ease my way along the cliff's edge to a lower point on the trail. It would require squeezing through some cactus bushes but doable.

I identified the maneuvers required to reach the lower trail but the descent down the cliff would be tricky. I would need both hands to balance myself alone the edge.

MOUNTAIN EDGE

I thought about the absurdity of my hat concerns given my present condition but afterall it was a gift from Alline. I couldn't imagine trying to explain what happened. So from my sitting position on the boulder I flung the backpack and trekking pole further down the trail towards the lower point I had identified.

It was time to get started.

After several visualizations of the maneuvers necessary for a safe descent I began to mentally prepare to get my meaningful hat.

My mind shifted back to Alline. This morning she texted me just before I got to Red Rock Canyon to remind me to pick her up from work at 7:00 p.m. This gave me plenty of time to drag myself back down the mountain.

While stealing more time to regroup, I checked my cell phone one last time for a reception. Nothing. But surprisingly another message had gotten through from my wife, *"OMG Kobe Bryant died today."*

KOBE BRYANT

Shaken, I asked God, "What was your purpose, on this day, in taking from this world a young brilliant father like Kobe and not an old earthly man like me?"

I did not hear an answer and having faith without answers is hard. But in God's silence I understood the truth. His purpose was shown in today's plight and I didn't recognize it until now. Kobe's journey was completed here on this earth and his spirit was called to the heavens to exist til infinity. On the other hand, God kept me alive because I was incomplete and still had work to do on this earth.

I was going to turn 65 years old in less than a month

and still had no idea what God had in store for me or what was going to make me complete so that I too could live in infinity. Only God knew the answer. All I had was faith and that would simply have to be enough.

A sense of foreboding began to creep into my head. Shaking it off, I no longer feared that my own death was imminent. But with such a daunting challenge ahead I knew that without God's help there was a strong possibility that Kobe and I would meet later today.

This was not the time to retrogress. God had already given me my life back and It was my job to believe that he will guide me through the wilderness. So I refocused all my energy on the struggle at hand.

Utilizing my gloved hands to push up, I stood slowly and methodically to prevent the possibility of losing my balance again.

MOUNTAIN TRAILS

It was going to be important from here on out to stay ahead of Murphy's Law. So I reassessed in my head each maneuver required to successfully retrieve the hat and safely make it back to the main trail.

The first maneuver to begin the descent would require me to roll on my stomach and carefully slide down the cliff to another boulder ten feet below. It was a move that I had used in the White Mountains of New Hampshire during my climb down the Flume Trail.

Once reaching the boulder and retrieving the hat I needed to pirouette to my backside. This maneuver was extremely risky because it would require me to be hands free even if only for a second. And Murphy had already proven that a second was more than enough time for him to bring disaster.

Yet it was a necessary risk to take in order to retrieve my hat. It would allow me to face out towards the horizon, gain the proper footing, and slide along the cliff wall to safety.

I wanted to immediately begin the descent while the necessary maneuvers were fresh in my mind. But Murphy said first I needed to catch my breath once again to decrease the dull pain in my chest and lessen the risk of failure.

'In and out, in and out, in and out'.

MOUNTAIN CLIFF

I moved closer to the mountain's edge. Then I stooped and twisted simultaneously to grab hold of the ground beneath me. I began easing myself down the cliffside.

Now that I had moved closer to the fallen hat I noticed that it was stuck on the thorn of a prickly pear cacti. GREAT! This eliminated the concern of accidentally knocking it further down the mountain's edge. Unabated, I was able to creep the rest of the way and retrieve my Stetson. Placing it on my head made me feel authentic again.

Hugging the mountain wall it was time for the

pirouette. Feeling a bit cocky, as if like Indiana Jones, I easily pirouetted to face the horizon. Then while sidestepping along the rocky brim towards the path Murphy quickly reminded me of his presence when my foot slipped off the cliffside. I was barely able to steady myself by grabbing the roots hanging out from the cliff-edge in a hope and prayer that they would hold my weight. They did. Allowing me to leap safely through the thorny bushes and land nearby the trekking pole.
My cockiness almost gave way to Murphy's Law. Or it might just have been pride before the fall. Either way it was another mistake. And yet another blessing.

The joy of success quickly turned into dismay as the exertion drained the energy from my body and I collapsed onto one knee. I feared that if I laid completely down I would never get back on my feet. Fighting through the dizziness and pounding heart was just less of impossible. Once again the animal inside me took control. I would need his survival instincts to make it back safely. I would also have to call upon all my skills as an experienced hiker. For example, following footprints on the path, locating obscure cairns, and utilizing my internal directional compass.

It was time to get my body moving once again. Leaning on the trekking pole for support while holding my backpack, I willed myself to stand on both feet.
Then I took a step. And another.
Success!
I needed to take a moment and slow my breathing before taking a third step.

'In and out, in and out, in and out'.

Dragging my backpack along, I moved at a snail's pace. Thank goodness God had gifted me with additional time today both figuratively and literally. The process of 'step, step, and rest' as my method of descent was working. I slowly began mitigating my way down the mountain.

During times of survival I find it fascinating that the mind will wander. I suspect it is a self-preservation mechanism the brain uses to prevent itself from being overcome by the fear of death. The problem is when you lose focus mistakes are made that can ultimately lead to your demise.

My mind began to wander again ...

I heard the chatter of the mountaineers as they inched their way up a distant cliff. The sounds of people talking, somewhere in my head, released Marvin Gaye, *"Brother, brother, brother there's far too many of you dying. You know we've got to find a way ...".*

Then I mentally floated into the realm of virtues that over time created my soul...

The seven virtues that I hold dear in this world are love, pain, sadness, happiness, adventure, beauty, and peace. Each of them represented a significant portion of my experiences in life. God and I hadn't had time today for a fruitful discussion of these topics. But they are why, in the end, my continuation of life has always prevailed over the choice of death.

From as far back as I can remember, the music that played in my head was the glue that allowed me to identify the seven attributes that were connected to my soul.

I could sit for hours listening to songs whose words and feelings touched my heart and shaped my desires. The lyrics I listened to influenced my entire being. And the depth of each song I would live in my dreams. Then subconsciously or consciously those dreams would become the actuality that I would choose to emulate. That is why I am known for saying, "I'm living the dream."

As if on cue, lyrics began to play in my mind, "*Master told me one day I'd find peace in every way. But in search for the clue wrong things I was bound to do.*

Keep my head to the sky for the clouds to tell me why ...". Singing was Earth, Wind, and Fire. *"He gave me the will to be free Purpose to live is reality ... so we're saying for you to hear keep your head in faith's atmosphere ...".*

With a stubbornly tenacious face I looked knowingly towards the sky. God's message was absolute. He was going to lead me out of this wilderness and home to the woman I revere. All I had to do was carry out my part of the covenant by keeping faith.

'In and out, in and out, in and out'.
Step, step, and rest.

Snapping back to the reality of the moment I looked around and there were no distinguishable landmarks. I shouted out loud, "Oh shit! My mind wandered!"

Scanning my memory bank, two hundred yards ahead along side the trail, I recognized a huge boulder with black and red streaks throughout. Another important detail used by experienced hikers because we understood the consequences of getting lost. These markers are used to determine time, location, and distance.

Realizing that I hadn't gotten very far, I decided to pick up the pace.

Step, step, step, step, and rest.

'In and out, in and out, in and out'.

The extra steps had cause my breathing to become more laborious. The dull pain in my chest felt aggravated so I took more time between taking in oxygen and taking another step. It meant that more time would be required to complete the descent but it was a necessary precaution.

Once again I lost focus and my attention to the now faded ...

Wandering about the events of the day I realized it had already encompassed all 7 of the virtues that reflect my inner soul. The LOVE for my wife, PAIN in my heart, SADNESS for Kobe, HAPPINESS doing what I truly enjoy, ADVENTURE in the wilderness, BEAUTY in God's creation, and PEACE in the face of death.

We go through life believing that time is on our side. Believing that once our career is established and we have achieved financial stability, the ability to enjoy our existence will come to fruition. Except we don't determine the time of our death.

In God's time, once our purpose is weaved into the cloth of infinity we leave our earthly body and our heavenly journey begins. Very rarely are we prepared to leave our loved ones behind.

Therefore it's important that we live every step of our life in the moment.

Of course, the concept of living in present is more difficult to do than say. The daily pressure we feel from societal norms, maintaining a quality standard of living, and our future desires has a way of controlling our thoughts. The focus on 'now moments' become almost impossible. It requires a mind shift against all your natural instincts based upon your teachings and experiences.

Yet to live within the daily journey of life brings us the greatest fulfillment of emotional, spiritual, and intellectual satisfaction. Imagine having the ability to live your dream every moment of the day every day of your life. It is pure happiness.

The lyrics of *'The Moment'* that was playing deep in my spirit came to the fore as the feeling of happiness came to my mind. Vargo sang, *"Now is the moment To let go of every burden that weighs me down. Open my mind releasing All my worries All my pain ... being one with all I am."*

I was never really sure which came first, the songs in my head or the living of my life. What I did know was that one could not exist without the other. I am certain that heredity and environment had to play a part in this way of relating to the world. My father had a passion for music so I grew up in a home surrounded by euphonious sounds.

Coupled with my mother's deafness, though she couldn't technically hear the sound, I suspect that music played in her head as they do mine. I was always amazed at how she moved perfectly to the beat when dancing with my father.

I had never truly connected the bond between mother nature, the sounds of music, and my dreams until this very moment. When all three came together they created the seven virtues that made me, me.

Step, step, and rest.

Oh shit. I had finally reached the first marker. I did not have the strength to climb atop the black and red boulder to seek the next marker. Luckily, I recognized my shoeprint in the sandy dirt path and knew that I was heading in the right direction.

I continued down the trail another half-mile dragging my backpack when I was jerked to a halt. The strap of my pack had gotten caught on a Joshua tree and would not pull free. After several dumb attempts of trying to jerk it loose I stumbled backward and almost fell onto a bed of Mountain balls. Angry with myself I slowly unattached the backpack and continued onward.

As I wandered and fussed to myself about the tree, one hundred yards later the trail became more narrow and difficult. It ended close to the mountain's treeline followed by a cliff edge with a steep drop-off to the valley below. It wasn't until then I realized that my inattentiveness had cost another mistake.

Discombobulated after fighting with the Joshua Tree I had continued in the same general direction but inadvertently taken an animal footpath and not the hiking trail.

Fatigue causes poor decision making and I had

forgotten to follow my shoeprints. Based on my current physical condition this mountain goat pathway was too difficult to descend to the valley. And backtracking just wasn't in the cards.

Walking towards the treeline I saw several areas where I could sit, drink, and formulate a strategy. I refused to sit for fear of not having the strength to get back up. So I Found a boulder that allowed me to simply lean back and relax under the shade of trees.

My body cooled as the wind blew and the sun rose towards midday.

Looking across the horizon and the steadfast beauty of the sun peaking out from a cloudy sky my spirit felt completely drained once again as the pain in my chest refused to vanish even while I wandered ...

Maybe I have it all wrong. Maybe this very moment is God's gift to me. Maybe this is to be my final resting point. I could not find Alline's face within the clouds anymore.

And though she had disappeared from my view I

continued to feel her presence as Vargo spoke, "The wind is whispering secret things Feel the silence deep inside ... Diving deep into your mind, you can let your soul unwind There's no fear to keep you down ... Trust yourself with your own sound Get back to serenity Tune yourself in to a true reality ...".

I felt the wetness on my cheeks as Vargo continued, "Peace of mind is all around Rising up when the sun goes down Into the ocean of your bliss Into the light where your home is ...".

Home. Alline.

I stood at the precipice of both Gunsight Notch and life. At this point, my survival had to rely upon the only thing I had left in my heart. The power of love.

Feeling her love inside me, I searched the clouds again for Alline's face knowing it had already gone. I sensed her protective spirit was nearby so I simply imagined her image into the sky. Her eyes, her nose, and her lips were inches from my face. The image spoke, "Come home to me."

Like a gentleman, I removed my Stetson and placed it

over my heart, leaned forward, closed my eyes, and kissed her dreamt lips. I'm not sure how but I could taste the sweet nectar in her mouth. The realness of the moment startled me and I pulled away as her face disappeared.

Placing my hat back on my head while laughing out loud I thought, *"I must be loosing my fucking mind."* Joyful delirium is a mindblowing trip and their memories continue to hold tight as gratifying experiences.

I had convinced myself years ago that my imagination of what love should be didn't exist in the real world. It was just a goal we all aspired to achieve knowing it was probably just a pipe dream. Real life always raised its all consuming head preventing the dream of total and complete happiness from ever reaching fruition.

On behalf of God, somewhere in the recess of my mind I could hear Mary Mary singing, *"Never said there wouldn't be trials. Never said I wouldn't fall. Never said that everything would go the way I want it to go. But when my back is against the wall and I feel all hope is gone, I'll just lift my head up to the sky and say help me be strong ...".*

My mind wandered deeper into the realm of love and survival.

I was wrong about everlasting love being just a dream. Minutes ago I was absolutely prepared to be welcomed into heaven but love intervened.

The virtue of LOVE is what moved inside me as my life slowly slipped away on Gunsight Notch. God had used the power of love as an instrument to protect me from death. It was love that gave me purpose and its strength cannot be underestimated. The emotions it can summon are more powerful and magical than any other human experience. It can find the strength within you that you didn't know existed. And without it we lose the ability to persevere when all else fails. When there's someone in life that has won our heart we choose to fight for existence in our abnigation of responsibility or even in the face of death.

I suspect that love's enchantment can be released not only because of the positve affection toward others but for the sake of self ... the ability to love thyself. It is truly an indescribable feeling. I imagine it's akin to being 'saved' in a religious sense.

Snapping back to my current situation, I already knew the answer was 'focus or lack thereof' when I asked myself, "How could I have gotten so far off track?"

I was too fearful of following the steep and slippery animal footpath down to the valley. And I absolutely wasn't going to backtrack. My instincts knew there was a better way down. I would just have to find it.

I dropped the backpack where I stood and leaned heavily against the pinyon pine tree that peeked gingerly over a ledge and down the valley wall.

It afforded me a view of the entire Pine Creek Canyon. While intently scanning the desert before me I began humming the song *'Crossroads'* and the lyrics rang in my head, *"Now tell me whatcha gonna do when there ain't nowhere to run ... God is who we praise even though the devil is all up in my face. He keeping me safe and in my place, say grace ... and we pray everyday everyday everyday ... standing at the crossroads ...".*

CAIRN

Then I saw it. To be sure I had to take a longer second look. Twenty-five yards away and barely visible was a small cairn. Looking through the thick brush I was amazed to find that the trail was close enough for me to see a chipmunk run across its path. The emotional relief I felt brought tears to my eyes. This was proof that God always shows himself when all else fails.

'In and out, in and out, in and out'.

It was time to get moving again.

Dragging my backpack I headed towards the main trail by using the trekking pole to push through the dense brush. With razor like focus I kept my eyes glued to its probable location. Once reaching the trail I realized that I was much further along than anticipated. The animal footpath was actually a shortcut and had moved me closer to the base of the mountain.

I hadn't got lost, God had simply given me a better path to take. I could not have been more blessed. The fearfulness of not surviving morphed into the thrilling challenge of an adventure. I was struck at how the mind can change your circumstances without your circumstances actually changing.

GUNSIGHT NOTCH

I stopped and turned to look back at Gunsight Notch. Its summit was a two time champion but I was not in the mood to crown it king. So at that very moment I vowed to return for a final showdown. It was simply against my constitution to concede. Even at my age. I vowed again to make a comeback and stand on the notch atop Gunsight Notch.

Above the treeline hiking is somewhat easier for me

because I am very adept at extrapulating the correct climbing technique from one point to the next. And because of my strong hands I am also skilled at utilizing my grip to maneuver past the larger boulders. My confidence was always tempered with the knowledge that the slightest slip and tumble could be much more devastating at the higher altitudes.

After 30 more minutes of slow methodical hiking while floating in and out of daydreaming I made it to the first of two Pine Creek Canyon valleys that I needed to cross before reaching the trailhead. Now I had to located the most doable means to the valley floor. The path with the most switchbacks leading down would eleviate the steepness and allow for an easier descent.

Though I was pleased to get below the treeline because it represented a landmark towards getting closer to safety, I didn't look forward to hiking down the steep walls of the Pine Creek valley. I always found it more difficult dealing with valley pathways and their slippery terrain.

PINE CREEK VALLEY

Unlike scrambling up or down the boulders of a desert mountain the steep traversing of a valley wall consisted of loose dirt, sand, and rocks. It required a good sense of physical balance and a proficiency with a trekking pole. One slight misstep could put you flat on your ass or hamper you with an ankle sprain.

Continuing to drag my backpack along was an obvious expression of my fatigue. This thought harkened the words of a radio commercial I produced years ago,

"When you look good you feel good."

So I struggled to shoulder my backpack and stand erect hoping that somehow it would strengthen my will as I continued towards the valley. It didn't. I quickly unshouldered the pack and commenced with the dragging again.

'In and out, in and out, in and out'.

I hadn't recently seen any indication of my whereabouts as I approached the first valley. Following the path along its upper edge I searched for a cairn that would signal the best trail location. Jumping back, I was half-startled by a Peregrine Falcon that was nesting close to the valley trail. I assumed it was the same falcon that I had a run-in with this morning. It had scared the bejesus out of me earlier but not now. I was too exhausted and my reaction time was nil.

Seeing the falcon was a good sign. It meant that I

must be near the exact path I ascended on my way to the Notch. Staring straight ahead I recognized the cairn that marked the way down to the valley. It was proof that I was halfway home.

I experienced a good tingling of the senses that acknowledged the adieu of dread from my soul.

In the wilderness, familiarity breeds confidence and confidence breeds positive energy. The extra burst of adrenalin was well received by my body.

'In and out, in and out'.

Step, step, and rest.

Just as I was about to descend, my solitude was disrupted by the sound of laughter. Approximately one hundred yards further along the upper edge of the valley wall were four hikers carrying a huge British flag. It looked as if they were taking pictures with their flag and using Gunsight Notch in the far distance as the backdrop. It was a very strange yet remarkable scene as they jumped around and sang the British

National Anthem.

It fleetingly crossed my mind to hike the additional yardage, approach the group, and ask for assistance. Unfortunately the sad truth of my reality in the wilderness, as in business and as in life, I simply didn't feel at ease about asking any white person for help. Not now and not ever. Particular to the wilderness they tend to assume that as a black man I'm an inexperienced hiker. Then I'll overreact by informing them that I've been hiking more years than they are old. Anyway, I didn't want to have to babysit my babysitters all the way back to the trailhead.

After a moment of watching the British hikers celebrate, I swung my backpack over my shoulder to free up my hand for better balance and stability. I could hear the Isleys in my head, *"From the highest mountain and valley low. We'll join together with a heart of gold ... I'm your brother. I'm your brother don't you know."*

Then I began my trek down the valley trail.

The words continued, *"We'll be living in a world of peace. In a day when everyone is free ... Won't you let your love flow from your heart."*

As my right knee buckled I immediately understood that the distractions of my mind was the immediate cause. Falling back with both feet in the air I psychologically prepared for the worst. But the trekking pole held my weight and I was somehow able to pull both feet back down before my butt hit the ground. Then I immediately placed my off hand on the ground to spring my body back up into a standing position ... almost perfect.

Murphy made sure I overshot the landing just enough to fall forward on my knees. I had to prevent myself from smashing my head so I released the pole to catch myself. It was the gloves that prevented me from completely scratching up my palms as I stopped myself from falling forward on my face.

I just held the ground position until my instincts gave way to mental calmness. Grabbing hold of the trekking pole again I was able to leverage myself and stand.

The remaining switchbacks leading down to the valley were not too steep but the ground was dry which made the loose rocks slippery. The trekking pole continued to saved my balance a few more times as I made it to the floor of the valley without major incident.

'In and out, in and out, in and out'.

Once down to the valley, I unshouldered my backpack so as not to hamper my breathing, got a drink of water, and took out the .38 for easy access. The valley is always more secluded with pockets of water at its base. Wilderness animals are more likely to be near those areas so a little prudence was necessary.

'In and out, in and out, in and out'.

RED ROCK CANYON AND SNOW CAPPED MOUNT CHARLESTON

I looked up and over Gunsight Notch at the snow capped mountains of Mount Charleston and Griffith Peak. Both stood ten miles away from my location. The melting snow flowed from those mountains down to the Pine Creek Canyon valley creating a wilderness densely populated with brush, cactus, and trees. The valley was wide and flat with the creek running through its center. It is here where I had to remain alert for mustangs, deer, and coyotes. A wild animal encounter was common place in the morning wilderness.

The peaceful nature of the valley and the sound of flowing water caused my mind to drift toward its

'Beauty' as Vargo sang, "*Find the face of beauty. The sound of waves ... A beaming face ... the silence at night ... Your tender touch. I open up my eyes and I'm amazed to find the face of beauty. A gentle voice ... the winds coress ... while being outside. So much to hear, to feel, to see. Each moment's a discovery to find the face of beauty ...*".

PINE CREEK

This was a surreal moment. As the music played in my head I could still hear the amplified sounds of wilderness around me. The hoot of an owl, the cooing of a morning dove, the scampering of chipmunks, and the unknown ruffling of bushes by the creek.

Dragging my backpack, I strolled to the beat in my head straight across the valley floor toward the creek as Vargas continued, *"Beauty is found in every step, in every sunrise, in every ray of sunlight that kisses my skin. The beauty of nature is very fragile ..."*.

Bushwacking my way through the thick brush, I approached the creek and came face to face with a doe. We both froze like a deer in headlights. I knew where there's one there's more.

After three eternity seconds of motionless staring she backed up slowly, turned, and walked away. With a fawn close behind she crossed the path ten feet in front of me and disappeared into the brush. Use of the .38 special never crossed my mind.

Challenging my climbing skills by facing off with perilous mountains was and is an addiction of pure pleasure. And on several occasions it nearly cost me my life. But to encounter a wild beast in the wilderness is an awfully close second. Both were breathtaking experiences.

This was turning into an adventure of a lifetime. My mind seemed to float in and out of consciousness while the pain in my chest throbbed between each heartbeat. Yet all around me was this beautiful and peaceful slice of heaven.

The time spent with God and the joy of bringing home an extraordinarily celestial spirit seemed worth the risk.

Step, step, and rest.
'In and out, in and out, in and out'.

After finding a safe place to cross the creek I headed towards the trailhead. I could feel God in my head reminding me to have faith that he would bring me safely back to Alline. I found it unusual for God to speak to me in the valley. Our conversations were generally reserved for the mountain tops but I guess he knew that something weighed heavily on my mind.

I asked aloud, "God why me? Why do I continue to deserve to live and others do not? Why do you make me fight for life time and time again? Why do you bring death to my door just to watch me slam it shut? Why did you take Kobe today when you could have had me?

Though he had given me the answer hours ago on Gunsight Notch I still struggled with understanding my worth in his eyes. I continued, "I don't attend church. I have serious questions about the validity of the Bible. I speak in the language of spirituality. I've also done some not so proud things in my life."

His answer remained the same, *"You still have a purpose on this earth."*

It didn't matter how much I felt undeserving of his blessings. I had to remind myself that it was not my place to judge but to have faith.

I tasted a salty liquid on my lips before realizing that tears flowing from my eyes.

'In and out, in and out, in and out'.
Step, step, rest.

Reaching the other side of the valley I shouldered the backpack and holstered the trekking pole. The trail out of the valley was approximately 60 feet and very steep. The loose gravel caused me to slip down several times on my earlier descent. It would be necessary to have the use all four of my limbs to crawl out so I would need both gloved hands free. This climb will put to test my current stamina but God had already reminded me who was in control.

Just before starting my climb out of the valley I was struck by exhaustion once again. My brain felt overheated so I removed my Stetson to let the morning breeze cool my head. The beating of my heart increased dramatically as if it was searching for more oxygen again. I was confused because at this altitude and with this plush landscape oxygen should be plentiful.

To control my pounding heart I closed my eyes to better concentrate on slowing down my breathing.

'In and out. In and out. In and out'.

ALLINE WALKER GRIFFIN

Distracting me from myself a life size image of Alline appeared. I watched while she danced in front of me. I recognized it as the moment I fell in love with her 10 years ago.

Shortly after we met, Alline and I had attended a basement house-party and she pole danced to Salt-N-Pepa, "Oh how you doin' baby ... What's your name, Damn that sounds sexy ... ah here I go, here I go again

... the brother had it goin' ... I couldn't believe this I swear, I stared ... I felt it in my hips so I dipped ... hell he makes me wanna shoop ...".

I continued with the vision of her sliding up and down one of the house foundation poles while wagging her finger for me to come to her.

I Laughed aloud as a breeze from the desert floor cooled my imagination. My heartbeat had slowed and my head had cooled. All I felt was love in my heart and pep in my step. I opened my eyes, slipped my hat back on, and climbed up the steep embankment without incident.

God is love.

ADVENTURE

Looking out over the horizon with my binoculars as I approached the final valley I could see the trailhead full of cars in the distance. No matter where you hike or how fatigued you may be, once you see the finish line you feel a sense of relief. It gives you the ability to relax your mind and focus totally on the physicality of completing the journey.

The ability to free my thoughts from the fear of death continued to allowed me to drift ...

Looking up at the sky the Bliss I felt and heard inside my head reminded me of how, with a single kiss, Alline helped me survive this day, "The sky is all I see it's never ending. We could fly you and I on a cloud, Kissing Kissing. On a journey of the heart and when the sky is dark you'll be right here with me, Kissing ...".

God had gifted me with more time to 'live the dream' with Alline and I was thankful.

Surviving all the trials and tribulations of this

adventure had almost drained the life out of me and I couldn't wait to get home and rest. My heart was full but that dull ache found it's way back inside my chest. It just wouldn't go away for any extended period of time. I began counting my footsteps as a distraction from the pain. Victory was near with less than one mile to reach the trailhead.

"In and out, in and out, in and out'.
Step, step, step, rest.

There were only a handful of times in my life where survival and death collided while in the mountain's wilderness. Over the years I had learned that once you allow the idea of failure to creep into your mind it almost always become inevitable.
My very first near tragic experience occurred at twelve years of age at summer camp. As a boy scout I would often sneak off alone and explore the wooded areas that were considered off limits. On one of many

excursions, in the middle of a swamp, I discovered a 10 foot narrow plank that led to a makeshift raft with a paddle. I walked the plank out to the raft. While paddling in the swamp a poisonous water moccasin raised up out of the water and rushed towards me flicking its forked tongue. As it lunged forward I swung wildly with the paddle and fell off the raft into the stagnant water. Landing feet first I waded to the safety of the shore with the water moccasin close behind. In that moment the fear, the exhilaration, and the challenge in the face of danger was breathtaking. And exciting. And fun. And scary. It felt natural and I felt at home in the wilderness.

As a kid hiking became a regular part of my routine whether I was at the neighborhood park, city park, or simply walking across an empty lot. In my mind's eye it was all an adventure of sorts and what dangers didn't exist I conjured up in my heart. Once I reached adulthood it became more than just a routine it was a way of life. I shifted from local and state parks to national parks. Then I began climbing mountains in an *effort to feed my thirst for more and more challenges.*

As I continued reminiscing on my very first risky mountain adventure, I could hear the Temptations in my head, *"You don't have to worry cause baby there ain't no mountain high enough Ain't no valley low enough Ain't no river wide enough to keep me from getting to you ... no wind no rain and winter's cold can't stop me ..." from reaching that mountain top.*

Still inexperienced as a climber I decided to tackle the difficult Flume Trail that led to the summit of Flume Mountain. It had already taken the life of an expert hiker earlier in the year.

It was a cloudy day with the possibility of light rain. Little did I know that the weather conditions were perfect for a climber's nightmare. Approaching the Flume Trail I completely ignored the heeding of another hiker who had decided to abort his attempt. I chalked it up to his fear and not being up to the challenge.

Starting the climb I immediately found rock climbing

up the Flume rather challenging but doable. I discovered that I was a natural at scrambling up the steep rock faces and my

confidence grew. Halfway up the mountain a slight drizzle started to fall which caused the rocks to become slippery. My lack of experience began to show itself. For starters tennis shoes are not suitable for inclement weather and the doable climbing changed to dubious climbing.

I was literally caught between a rock and a hard place. It was too dangerous to turn back and too difficult to continue climbing. There I sat, waiting for the rain to stop so I could continue the journey. Except the rain didn't stop and two hours later time became a factor and I was forced to make a decision. So I chose to continue climbing up to the peak.

The trail traveled up the slick wall of a sheer cliff that required adept climbing skills. Skills that I had yet to acquire. My lack of ability coupled with water flowing down the cliff made the way up or down a treacherous climb.

I threw my backpack and hiking stick up 10 feet to the landing ledge above the sheer rock cliff. Bending my knees to thrust myself, I leaped up the cliff to grab hold of the ledge.

I missed.
As I slid down the mountainside towards my death the tips of my toes caught hold of an unseen indentation in the cliff wall and stopped the free fall. I hugged onto the cliff for dear life. With unbridled fear I remained frozen, pressed against the wall with rain water streaming down my face and body. I could not believe my good fortune or God's blessing. Or both.

The passing of time eventually ushered in a sense of calm and the gravity of the current situation eventually caused the fear to become replaced by possibility. Then possibility was replaced by determination. Then determination was replaced by will ... the will to live.

Clarity of the moment came into focus and I saw other indentations that led up the steep cliff. My mind's eye pictured a pattern within the formation. With no experience in rock climbing through the perilous flow of rain I methodically inched my way up to the landing and lifted myself over the ledge to safety. In that instant I had progressed from being a novice to having experience as a hiker.

I stood on the peak of Flume Mountain and thanked God for giving me the courage and strength to survive this adventure. And through my heart He spoke to me for the first time. I cannot explain or express how God spoke to me but he was pleased that I had faith in him.

This was the first of many heartfelt conversations to come.

Step, step, step and rest.

'In and out, in and out, in and out.'

Prince whispered in my ear as I methodically crossed the valley, "Here we are staring each other down. You want me just as much as I want you. Let's stop fooling around ... Baby you know that's all I been dreaming of ... I want you so bad."

Being struck by humor, I smiled because sexual thoughts is not what played in my mind. Of all things, the song in my head reminded me of the first time I spoke directly to a mountain. While standing at the base of Old Speck and staring at its summit I told him that I had dreamed about climbing him so we needed to stop fooling around and do the damn thing. I wanted him bad ... just like the song.

The echo of my laughter bounced off the canyon walls and filled the valley. And as more laughter filled the Pine Creek valley my drifting continued ...

Step, step, step, step, step.

It was a very beautiful and clear 60 degree day with a slight breeze. Unusual for the month of April in the Northeastern part of the country. After canoeing the Androscoggin River in Gilead Maine I decided to get an early start the following day and go hiking. Looking at the map, I decided on Old Speck Mountain once again. It is the tallest of the Mahoosuc Range and the trail is only recommended for very experienced adventurers particularly in the snow months. The kind of challenge dreams are made of.

As I approached Old Speck the low lying clouds hid the summit. It was of fleeting concern because the snow on the ground had all but disappeared. Therefore I didn't see a need for snow shoes.

By the time I had ascended two miles up the steep trail the temperature dropped below freezing and snow flurries started falling from the partly sunny sky. It was beautiful to witness.

And with humor from an old folklore I just thought that 'the devil was beating his wife'.

In just a matter of minutes darkened clouds appeared and the sun vanished behind them. The light flurries quickly changed to rather large flakes and the trail was completely covered within minutes.

I was surprised to find several inches of snow and ice

still in the higher elevations and wished I'd worn my snow shoes. Instead of the hiking stick I should have also brought my trekking pole. It has a much sharper metal point that can penetrate the ice for stability. The icy snow continued to deepen. With only a half-mile left to reach the peak I felt fairly confident that it was achievable.

Completing the last switchback before the summit I could see the observation tower that sat atop the peak. The trail was extremely close to the cliffside so I peered down the mountain and it seemed to drop off into a blinding fog.

The last 50 feet up was a steep and very slippery slope. There were several occasions when I lost my footing and grabbed hold of a shrub to stop myself from sliding back down the incline. A risky move to make because there is no guarantee that the shrub is securely grounded.

When I finally reached the tower the clouds above it appeared ominous and the snow fall turned into a *blizzard. I climbed the wooden tower to get a view of the entire valley but the snowfall was too dense and the sky was starkly invisible. It was twelve noon but it looked as if the sun had already set.*

I instinctively knew that I was in trouble.

The weather had changed faster than I had ever seen and I was ill-prepared to make the trek back down the mountain. My anxiety increased exponentially as the fear in my stomach move up to my throat.

By the time I had climbed down the observation tower the snow on the peak was knee deep and the trail had disappeared underneath.

The entire summit was blanketed with snow and I could not recall from memory the exact location of the trail. Knowing that uncertainty in the mountains can be disastrous I firmed up my intrepidness. Utilizing my hiking stick for balance I reached the steep incline where I had imagined the trail down probably began. In order to survive on this ice-capped mountain time was of the essence and even it seemed inconsequential.

As a hiker I had learned to rely on my instincts and I would do so once again atop Old Speck. I felt the addictive adrenalin rush from the thrill of a challenge and smiled. I knew death was near. Ill-suited, I sat on my butt and began slowly sliding down the mountain.

Step, step, rest.

'In and out, in and out, in and out.'

Floating in and out of daydreaming my memory of the past came into focus and I heard Mystical in my ears, "You know what time it is nigga ... Danger ... watch yourself or fuck around and get beside yourself ...".

Laughing, all I could say aloud was, "Please God help a nigga out." as I drifted back ...

I heard the faint chirp of a Yellow Warbler. To my left through the blowing wind and falling snow I could see the bright yellow bird perched on a tree branch. He flew from one branch to another just a few feet away.

The fog lifted from my memory and I realized that the Warbler was flying directly over the actual trail and I was sliding directly towards the cliffside. I regained my focus and could visualize the drop-off just five feet ahead on the icy slope. One more slide without a trekking pole and I would have disappeared down the mountain.

God had spoken to my heart through the chirp of a bird. The Warbler sang as it flew from branch to branch along the snow covered trail leading me down the mountain. Once we reached a lower altitude the blizzard dissolved into flurries and the trail was visible once again. With gratitude I looked for the Yellow Warbler but he had already disappeared.

'In and out, in and out, in and out'.
Step, step, rest.

In my minds eye I could see myself making progress as the valley wall drew close and I drifted ...

Angels Landing is considered one of the top ten most dangerous hikes in the United States. An average of three hikers per year fall to their death. I was excited about the prospects of such an adventuresome hike. Alline decided to join me on this journey. This meant that anything dangerous would be kept to a minimum. If I contemplated a decision that she perceived as remotely troublesome her vote would be 'absolutely not'.

Still, Utah is a state full of wonder and I had the feeling that we were in for a thrilling experience.

ANGELS LANDING TRAIL

It was a perfect day for hiking. The Angels Landing Trail began by crossing the lazy flowing Virgin River in Zion National Park. We hiked the well marked trail up a steep mountain with numerous switchbacks. The views were spectacular as we continued up the steep incline towards Refrigerator Canyon.

The mountain wilderness was full of scenic beauty that kept our minds off the difficult hike. It naturally gave us opportunities to rest while taking photos of the view.

We reached Refrigerator Canyon and found it to be appropriately named. The high canyon walls kept the trail shaded from the sun which kept the canyon cooled. We hiked a half-mile through the less strenuous Refrigerator Canyon before reaching Walter's Wiggles.

It is one mile of twenty one very steep switchbacks leading up to the commanding views of Scout Lookout. Our trekking poles were a life saver as we *methodically climbed the Wiggles while occasionally catching opportunities to stop and rest.*

Scout Lookout was the base camp for those hikers who chose not to climb the deadly narrow section of the mountain to the summit.

Alline and I agreed that she would wait for me at Scout Lookout as I chose to continue climbing.

I had taken note early in our hike that the higher altitude was causing me an unusual shortness of breath. Though I was a bit surprised I still maintained a high degree of confidence as I began the climb. I just had to be more aware of my body's reactions and take appropriate measures.

Step, step, rest.

'In and out, in and out, in and out'.

SCOUT LOOKOUT

PASSAGE TO SUMMIT

The final passage to the summit of Angels Landing was dangerously steep and narrow with sheer cliff drop-offs. There were roped chains strategically placed by the drop-offs to assist with the ascent. Without them I had no doubt more hikers would have plummeted to their death. With the exception of Mount Lafayette I had never climbed such a narrow ridge in my 45 years of hiking. It was exhilarating. The views were only matched by those White Mountains of New Hampshire.

Out of nowhere exhaustion struck me halfway up the Landing. I could not catch my breath so I assumed it was the altitude. Stepping away from the drop-off I sat heavily on the pathway and laid my back against the mountainside. I understood that part of the challenge in climbing mountains was my body adjusting to the altitude. Having experienced fatigue in the past I had a good understanding of what to expect but I didn't recognize this extreme level of exhaustion. I had already climbed beyond what was halfway to the peak and nothing on this earth was going to prevent me from reaching the summit. After a 10 minute recovery period it was time to resume hiking. Leaning against my trekking pole for support I adjusted my backpack and began again.

Fifteen minutes later exhaustion caused me to stop and recuperate before starting again. I stopped and started three more times before reaching the summit.

SUMMIT ANGELS LANDING

I have never been deterred from the unknown challenges that one has to face in the mountain's wilderness. The adventure of it all gives my life real meaning. It fills my heart and brings me closer to God.

Collapsing at the peak of Angels Landing I thanked God for allowing me to get through this ordeal and completing the journey. The 360 degree view was the most beautiful I had ever imagined. Pulling out my cellphone to capture the stunning mountain landscape I saw a text from Alline, "Come back to me."

So I did.

VIEW FROM ANGELS LANDING

With focus I saw one more rather easy glen to cross before reaching the Pine Creek Trailhead. I tried to pick up my pace but to no avail.

My exhaustion exceeded the exhilaration so I continued to drag my backpack while hiking in survival mode. No one could know how exasperated I felt at this very moment but me and Tony Rich, *"I'm dying inside and nobody knows it but me. Like a clown I put on a show the pain is real even if nobody knows. I'm crying inside and nobody knows it but me ..."* Tony Rich continued in my mind, *"I carry a smile when I'm broken in two...I'm trembling inside and nobody knows it but me...my heart is calling you but nobody knows it but me ...".*

'I'm dying inside' was the only way to describe my thoughts. Even with the strength of my faith in God and the power of my love for Alline doubt continued to creep into my psyche.

The desire for life and the thieving of death were engaged in a ferocious fight for control of my body.

'In and out, in and out'.

Step, step, and rest.

Approaching the final valley I heard the laughter of children. This was music to my ears because it meant that this arduous journey was coming to an end and the fight was almost over.

At this point the trail had widened and was much easier to identify. The trail leading down to the valley was well worn and easy to descend.

I ran into a family walking their dog and in an effort to not appear distressed I shouldered the backpack and straightened my back. I remembered what my brother Charles would always say, "Pride before the fall." But I didn't care on this day as I held my head up high. Walking past the family I casually nodded, spoke, and continued on my way.

It is interesting how extraordinary strength can be drawn from unknown parts of the soul. I had gone from feeling totally beaten to projecting total confidence in just a matter of seconds.

The closer I got to the end of my journey more hikers and tourists passed by me on the trail. The last 50 yards to the trailhead was all uphill and I couldn't go any further without some type of sustenance. So I unshouldered the backpack and found a nearby large rock to sit and relax. I pulled an apple from my backpack. It was truly a struggle to continue lifting my arm each time I took a bite. Exhaustion had taken its toll on my body.

After completing the final 50 yards my adventure had come to an end. With tears of joy I walked over to the SUV and opened the trunk. I tossed in the backpack and trekking pole. Then took the time to dust off my Stetson and change shoes because Alline doesn't like it when I dirty up the floorboard.

Afterwards, I walked to the driver's side door and fell into the driver's seat totally spent of all energy. And there I sat for 15 minutes thanking God for bringing me out of the mountain wilderness safely and thanking Alline for her love.

Today's adventure in Red Rock Canyon was not about the climbing of Gunsight Notch. It was about ascending the mountain of faith and believing in love in order to defeat the unexpected whispers of death. A battle whos dull pain continued to rage in my heart.

I just needed to drive home and rest. Little did I know that my journey had just begun.

PAIN

The dull pain in my chest would not subside as I drove out of Red Rock Canyon. I listened to Telepopmusik on Pandora, "... You haunt my dreams There's nothing to do but believe. Just believe. Just breathe. Just believe. Just breathe. Another day, just believe. Another day, just breathe."

'In and out, in and out, in and out'.

Though it was only a 15 minute trip home, while on Interstate 215, I seriously thought about pulling over just to close my eyes for a minute and rest. But the idea of stopping on the highway raised my antenna and felt concerning. I suppose that pulling off the road to rest was akin to confessing that something was severely wrong with me physically and my inner being was not yet ready to make that jump.

I made it home without incident.

I stood looking up the 17 steps I had to climb in order to reach the second floor and take a shower. It reminded me of a time when my 82 year old deaf mother in semi-jest signed, *"And every day I would just stand and look up at those 17 steps it took to get to the kitchen ..."*. My humor was derived from my mother and I laughed a hardy laugh at our shared perspective. You know that you are tired when you find yourself counting the number of steps to climb.

As always after a hike, I decided feeling better would come after taking a hot and relaxing shower. It was more difficult than usual to undress, get in the shower, and clean myself. The exhaustion was almost unmanageable. I had to sit on the side of the bathtub every minute just to regain some semblance of normality.

I decided to do the laundry in hopes that normal behavior would allow me to will myself into good health. It didn't work.

Listening to the music of Banzai Republic I fell into the bed hoping that 'Sleep Will Come'. I Closed my eyes to rest but the dull pain in the center of my chest made it impossible to sleep as the violin solo hauntingly played.

As I laid in bed, I realistically thought maybe, just maybe, something might be wrong with my heart. This revelation stoked the fear whose fire was obviously laying dormant deep in my psyche.

The ideal that me, a mountain man, might no longer be so virile was disheartening. It required a new way of viewing today's entire set of events. Making my exhaustion only the side effect of a much larger problem. I slowly began to realize that my invincibility might not be so invincible. As my anxiety increased my heart began beating faster causing the pain in my chest to intensify.

The one thing that I did learn in the wilderness this morning was how to survive the intense pain in my chest. It required gaining control of my breathing and my will to survive.

'In and out, in and out, in and out'.

I decided that it would be prudent to go to the hospital and get checked out. I did not want to go to the emergency room alone so I called Alline at work. Very calmly, I explained my physical concerns and asked if she would take off work early to accompany me to the emergency room. I could hear the sound of panic in her voice as she questioned my somewhat cavalier decision to 'pick her up' instead of calling 911 immediately. With a soothing voice to hide my very real fear of not wanting to go alone I reassured her that this was just a precautionary measure.

LUXOR EMPLOYEE ENTRANCE

I got dressed and drove to the Luxor employee entrance. Alline insisted on driving when I picked her up.

Holding hands, we entered the emergency room at Spring Valley Hospital. A sign just left of the entrance read 'If you are experiencing chest pains please notify the receptionist at the front desk immediately'.

Your Care Team

Admitting Physician - Rosenberg MD, Murray M
Attending Physician - Rosenberg MD, Murray M
Consulting Physician - Janga MD, Radhika
Rosenberg MD, Murray M
Sharma, Deepak MD
Umakanthan DO, Branavan

Primary Care Physician - Chaney MD, Naomi L
Referring Physician - No, Pcp No MD

Reason for Your Visit

CP started today. Pt states was hiking at Red Rock this morning, felt dull pain, then went home to rest. Took aspirin. Pain didn't go away. Hx: HTN (takes meds)

Your Diagnosis

Acute kidney failure, unspecified
Benign hypertension
Chest pain
Chest pain
Non-ST elevation MI (NSTEMI)
Obesity
Renal insufficiency

SPRING VALLEY HOSPITAL

So we approached the receptionist and I calmly stated, "Your sign at the front entrance said I should notify you if experiencing chest pains. Well I have a dull pain in my chest." The receptionist immediately asked me to sit in the chair next to her desk. I sat and Alline stood behind my chair with her hands on my shoulders.

The receptionist called over a nurse to take my blood pressure. After getting a normal reading I was ushered over to another chair and the receptionist instructed another person to start the process of checking me into emergency.

He asked, "On a scale of 1 to 10 what is your pain level?"

I answered, "Well maybe a six."

He took my personal information and found my name already in the system. I recently had prostate surgery in the same hospital.

He then asked, "What happened?"

My response, "I was hiking up at Red Rock Canyon on my way to Gunsight Notch Peak and I started having chest pains. I fell then got up and dragged myself down from the mountain and came here."

He stated, "We're going to need to take blood tests. You drove here after climbing down the mountain? Man you're lucky."

Me, "Well first I showered, then washed clothes, then picked my wife up from work."

He stared at me then looked at Alline. She simply nodded her head.

He moved us into a small room, adjacent to emergency, where they take blood samples. Another nurse asked what happened. I explained once again about Red Rock Canyon. She told me how blessed I must be as she attempted to find a vein ripe for sticking.

Alline, standing by my side, informed her that I was a difficult stick.

She seemed fairly confident that it was a non-issue for her ability and said, "Your bloodwork should take about 15 minutes. We'll call you when it's done."

Fifteen minutes later I was called back to the room. A

doctor with my paperwork in hand said, "Well you definitely had a heart attack. The normal Troponin I level is 0.0 to .04. Your Troponin level is 4.7 which is critical. This only occurs when there's been a heart attack.

Alline asked, "What is Troponin?"

He responded, "It's a protein that measures heart damage. You also have acute kidney failure. I read the report that you were hiking. How did you get here?"

The room had fallen silent and everyone in the room just stared at me as I explained once again about hiking at Red Rock.

With a quizzical look the doctor stated, "Well you're extremely ... we're going to need to keep you here overnight. Is this your wife?"

Alline and I spoke simultaneously, "Yes. Overnight?" It was a subject that we had discussed on the drive to the hospital but I had not accepted this reality as a possibility.

Him, "Yes. First we'll have to free up a bed in ICU so just

be patient. It shouldn't take long. Are you in pain?"

Still trying to absorb the prognosis I said, "Just a bit of tightness in the chest."

"While you're waiting, we're going to take your EKG and have it ready for the Cardiologist." He smiled, turned, and walked away.

Alline and I just stared at each other and our silence spoke volumes. Obviously they all knew something that we didn't and that was worrisome. But if another person looks at me like I just escaped from the morgue I'm going to scream.

Sitting in the waiting room contemplating what just happened was surreal. When you have to examine your mortality life takes on a different meaning.

I heard Enigma creeping into my head, "... quem quaerimus adjutorem, nisi te, Domine ... take a deep breath ... and relax ... I look inside my heart ... I look inside my soul ... and when the lamb opened the seventh seal ...".

This could not be the end of my time. This could not be my revelation. God had not brought me down from the mountain and the rivers of belief just for me to rest in peace. There was a greater purpose and I just had to have faith.

I looked at Alline next to me texting on her phone and simultaneously the music from Thievery played inside my soul, *"I want to do is stay ... I came back to you, I love you, My angel wife. No worry grows. Everything will work out fine ... My heart waits for you ...".*

In a trance of an unbelievable sort I slowly scanned the entire emergency room full of patients. Young, old, and somewhere in between. Each of us struggling within our own thoughts, feelings, and prayers.

Angela's music filled my head again because it was hard to 'Breathe', *"There's nothing to do but believe, Just believe, Just breathe. Another day, just believe. Another day, just breathe. Another day, just believe. Another day, just breathe. I'm used to it by now. I'm used to it by now. Just believe. Just breathe. Just believe."*

Awakened out of my unconsciousness when I heard my name being called, I saw the nurse waving me into the next room. Alline grabbed my jacket, her purse, and followed me to the door. I slowed so she could enter first ... it was the gentleman thing to do.

As we walked through the hospital the nurse spoke, "We have your private room ready just follow me back. You'll spend the night here. We'll need to draw more blood, prepare your IVs, get you hooked up on oxygen, and get your medication."

As we entered the private room, somewhere in the recess of my mind I could hear Alline asking questions but I was completely numb to my immdiate surroundings. As the vision of snow cap mountains rushed past I could only, with clarity, hear Vargo,

"Now is the moment to let go, of every burden that weighs me down. Open my mind releasing all the worries all my pain ...".

The nurse's voice continued, "Here is your gown. You'll need to get undressed and the doctor will be in shortly to explain everything. Are you going to stay with him overnight? Good. This is a sleeper chair and I'll bring you a pillow and blanket." Vargo continued, *"Far away, I soar away, I float away, I fly away ...".* Then nothing but the sounds of music played in my head as I felt weightless and boundless being one with all I am. Everything was completely in God's hands now.

After undressing, I layed in the hospital bed while nurses came in and out. First an IV in my left arm. Then an IV in my right arm. Oxygen intake slipped up my nose. Take this pill. Take your blood pressure. Take your temperature. Blankets placed over my body. Television remote placed in my hand. Laughter and light talking.

I smiled at hearing Alline's voice, "I'm going to go home and change out of my work clothes. I'll be back."

Me, "You don't have to spend the night. I'll be okay. "

All of my adult life I have never depended on anyone doing anything involving my personal health and no one in my life ever volunteered. I was used to never being loved that deeply. My illnesses were always faced alone.

Alline stared at me in disbelief, "You crazy. Of course I'm spending the night. And every night as long as it takes. I would never leave you alone."

Blinking quickly to hold back my tears from the joy of being loved so amorously, I tried to respond nonchalantly, "Oh. Okay." But I knew she knew my truth.

Leaning over me, she whispered, "I love you hunbun."

Then she squeezed my hand and kissed my lips before leaving.

Over the years I was always the one in a relationship that did the extra work and stayed the extra mile through the healing process of the significant other. It was never reciprocated nor expected to be. I always felt that my love ran deeper than most and it was unrealistic to expect someone else to understand the fullness of true love. At least, until I met Alline. God had granted me the only gift I ever asked of a partner; to simply love me.

I learned that love can even supersede pain. The love my heart felt in that moment when her lips kissed mine took away all the pain that I was experiencing up to that point. Closing my eyes I could hear Babyface, "It's been a long time coming but it's been worth the wait ... It feels like heaven has opened up its gates for me and you. Every time I close my eyes I thank the Lord that I got you ... I can't believe that someone like you Loves me too."

The nurse came in again and asked about my pain level.

I answered, "zero."

Alline came back through the door with her smile and dancing eyes. She walked directly to me and once again grabbed my hand and kissed my lips. I became woke. I already knew that she was special but was taken aback by her strength during a crisis. She is a woman not fond of blood or the hospital environment yet there was no display of uneasiness. God works in mysterious ways.

Then I realized that today's ordeal may not have even been about me at all. Instead, it might be about Alline and her show of strength during a crisis. Or about our daughter Kristin and not taking life for granted. Or our future grandbaby who will have a story to tell as President of the United States. Or a hundred years from now I'll be smiling in heaven for it could be any one of these reasons. Or one I'll never know about.

And that is where our faith enters the story. For without our faith in God we are nothing.

The head doctor on duty appeared with my chart in hand and introduced himself, "I'm Doctor Rosenberg. Looks like you had a little heart attack. We'll keep you monitored tonight. Then tomorrow we're gonna have to go in and take a look at your heart to see what's going on. It's an unobtrusive procedure. Dr. Umakathan, your surgeon, will go in through the groin with a camera and take a look. We're hoping that it will only require a stent. If so, he can take care of it right away. Any questions?" Alline spoke, "So it won't require open heart surgery?"

Doctor Rosenberg responded, "Well we won't really know until we go in and take a look but let's hope it doesn't come to that. Doctor Umakathan is one of our best cardiologist so you'll be in good hands." He then left the room. Doctors always seem in a hurry.

The words 'little heart attack' and 'hope it doesn't come to that' seemed a dichotomy. It did not instill confidence in my survival and caused the pain in my heart to return.

I could feel Alline's tension and tried to ease her thoughts, "Well that was interesting."

She responded, "I don't like him."

I suppose it was something about his bedside manner, or just being the bearer of bad news, or his rather sloppy appearance. Either way we both felt some kind of way. It was going to be a long night.

The nurse came in shortly thereafter displaying an excited disposition, "Oh my God you got the best cardiologist in Las Vegas doing the surgery! Dr. Uma is great! Just ignore the long hair." She continued, "We'll be checking up on you every couple of hours throughout the night. Would you like something to eat? I'll let the attendant know."
Me, "Yes thank you."

DR. BRANAVAN UMAKANTHAN, DO INTERVENTIONAL CARDIOLOGY

Alline googled up Dr. Branavan Umakanthan to see his photo and read his reviews. He indeed had long hair and his reviews were exceptionally excellent. With a bit of skepticism our confidence slowly returned and the pain in my chest eased. It was time to sleep.

It was a restless night. Nurses in and out to check this and that. The monitors occasionally sounding their alarm whenever I shifted in the bed causing the nurse to rush into the room. Alline and I speaking about the surreal nature of the entire ordeal and how incredibly blessed I was to be alive. Morning couldn't come fast enough. We were both tired, restless, and full of anticipation.

I immediately recognized him from the Google photo as he walked into the room and spoke, "Hi I'm Dr. Umakathan but most people just call me Doctor Uma. I'll be doing the procedure today."
Alline stated, "Well we've heard nothing but great

things about you so I'm depending on you to keep my husband alive."

Dr. Uma responded, "I promise to do my best. My nurse will be in shortly to escort you down to O.R."

There was an aura about his demeanor that felt authentic and we both nodded to reassure ourselves and him of our faith in his ability.

January 27, 2020 at 2 p.m. It was time.

"Hi I'm Doctor Uma's head nurse and I'll be taking you down for your procedure. Before we go I have a few questions to ask."

After completing her list of questions about my understanding of what was going to happen next she gave me an authorization form to sign giving Dr. Uma the ability to do whatever it takes to save my life.

I was wheeled out of the room and to the elevator. As we passed by the nurse's desk every one wished me well. Doctor Uma was waiting for us by the operating room door. With an air of confidence he told us not to worry.

Alline told me that she loved me, kissed me, and headed to the waiting room. I told her that I loved her more and was wheeled into the operating room.

Waiting for me were three nurses that welcomed me into the room and rolled my bed next to the operating table.

After sliding onto the operating table my bed was quickly removed and the nurses went to work. One was explaining the process of inserting the camera into my groin artery and putting dye into my bloodstream. The other was shaving my groin area and prepping it for the procedure. The third nurse was attaching oxygen to my nose and inserting anastesia into my IV.

I could hear them telling jokes as they worked. I suggested that they watch what was being said because I'm writing a book about this entire experience. Laughter filled the room and I continued to watch and listen as they prepared me for the procedure.

I felt pressure in the groin area and tensed up. I heard a voice tell me that if I just relax it won't hurt as much. So I breathed.

'In and out, in and out, in and out'.

I continued to hear the nurses laughing as they discussed their kids and family life.

Then a nurse asked, "How do you feel?"

I answered, "Not bad so far. Just ready to get started."

She smiled and stated matter of factly, "Oh. Actually we're done."

I laughed at what was assumed a joke.

She reiterated, "No. Actually we are done."

I responded, "But I haven't seen Doctor Uma yet."

She answered, "He's in the waiting room talking with your wife. Everything went well."

I had difficulty putting it all into perspective. My mind was telling me that I was awake the entire time so I couldn't have missed the surgery. Looking at the clock on the wall, somehow an hour had past that was unaccounted for.

Then the chills began. They moved me off the operating table, back onto my bed, and wheeled me out of the operating room. Alline was standing just outside the room and greeted me with a smile and kiss.

Then she spoke, "Doctor Uma said everything went well. I love you. How do you feel?"

I was still shaking from the cold air when I spoke, "I can't believe it's over. I'm freezing."

I heard someone say, "We'll get you a warm blanket just as soon as we get to your room."

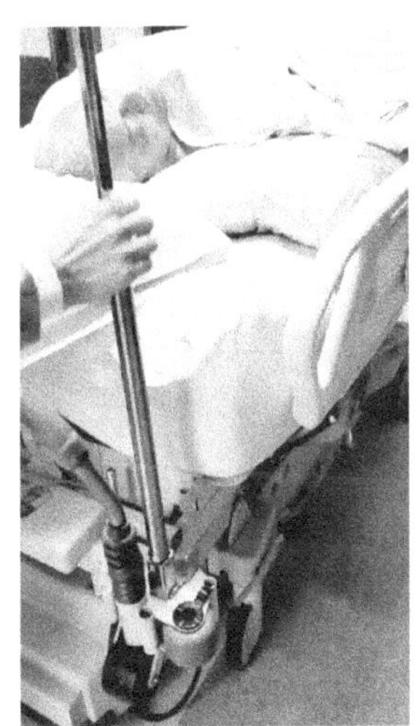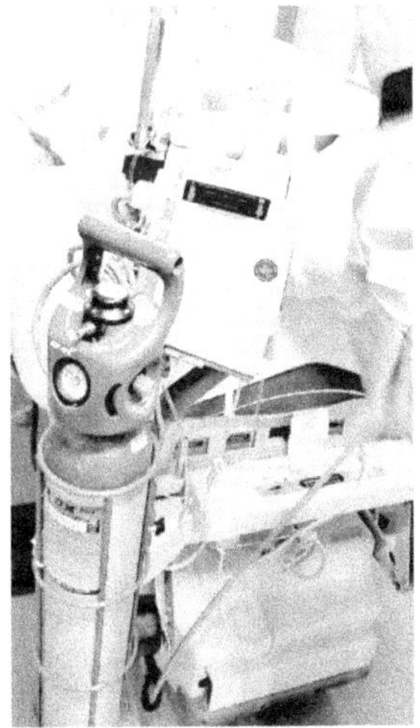

HEART SURGERY

Shortly thereafter we were back in my private room with nurses all around hooking me back up to the monitor, oxygen, and IV fluids. Then the nurses left the room. Always wearing her feelings on the sleeve I could see a look of concern on Alline's face. It was time to talk.

The dull pain in my chest returned.

Alline spoke, "Well there's good news and bad news. You had 100% blockage in your right artery and a stent was put in. But you have 80% blockage in your left artery and that will require a second procedure. The dye they use to identify the blockage is extremely hard on the kidneys. So Doctor Uma only used it in the right artery. It will need to be flushed out of your kidney before he can do the left artery."

Me, "Oh. Because of the acute kidney failure?"

Alline, "Yep. We'll have to come back at a later date to complete the procedure."

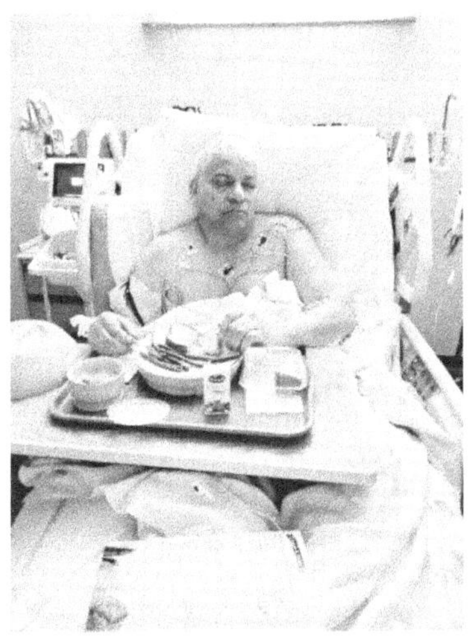

I'm not sure what I had hoped for but I suppose things could have been worse. I was not eager to spend another night in the hospital yet I understood that it was a necessary precaution.

Doctor Uma stopped by the room and we had the opportunity to thank him for keeping me safe. He agreed to release me from the hospital in the morning if everything seemed normal overnight. So Alline and I spent another restless night at the hospital.

Speaking to the morning nurse I asked, "The pancakes, eggs, and bacon was delicious. Now what time do I get to go home? I was informed that just as soon as Doctor Rosenberg stopped by and gave the okay we would be discharged."

As if right on cue Dr. Rosenberg stepped into the room, "Everything looks good. How do you feel?"

Me, "I'm doing great. Just ready to get going."

I recieved authorization to be released from the hospital. After helping me get dressed Alline left to get the car ready. As the nurse's aid wheeled me down the hall to the elevator all the RNs wished me the best. I made clear that I hoped not to see them again. We laughed as they agreed with my statement. Walking through the front door of our apartment was like a fog being lifted from my mind bringing back a sense of needed reality. Like a mother hen Alline put me straight to bed while she took care of things around the house.

We hadn't got much sleep the last couple of days. After a few hours and some coaxing on my part Alline decided to join me in bed. We held each other closely and spoke softly about our love before falling asleep.

It wasn't until the next morning that we woke. I instinctively turned on my favorite Pandora station for morning music. After a light breakfast we sat across from the other on bar stools and shared our thoughts. Discovering that we were both still sort of numb about the whole turn of events in our life. We agreed that the most beautiful thing about discovering nature's way of living is understanding that every day represents a new beginning. To live each day as if it were your last ... an opportunity for gratitude, beatitude, and serenity.

Listening to the music on Pandora Alline held out her hand and asked me to dance. I nodded, grabbed her hand, and pulled her body close to mine. I felt her relax in my arms and it reminded me of our wedding day.

Robin Thicke sang, "Cause when you love somebody, and need somebody ... so help me help you love. I don't care. I don't care. Anytime, anyplace, anywhere. Don't it sound like a sweet romance."

In the middle of our living room floor I held her hand and we began slow dancing as Robin continued, "You make me want this night to last forever ... love is never easy. Your love I'm never leaving ...".

I trembled slightly and she held me tighter. I did not want her to know me vulnerable but I was certain that when we kissed my lips tasted of salt from the tears.

Pulling back just a bit Alline looked up into my eyes and whispered, "I got you."

Two days later it was time for our appointment with Doctor Uma. While we waited in the exam room the nurse took my blood pressure and temperature, and completed an EKG.

Dr. Uma walked into the exam room with a quizzical look, leaned in towards me and said, "Now, you know that you had a significant heart attack right? How do you feel?"

I answered, "Well, I felt great until just a minute ago when you used the word 'significant'."

We all laughed uneasily.

After a review of his exam we found that my heart was responding in a positive manner. Alline explained to Doctor Uma that we wanted the next procedure to be sooner rather than later. So it was scheduled for two weeks.

On January 30, 2020 after arriving home from Doctor Uma's office we listened to the afternoon MSNBC news about a newly discovered virus in China called coronavirus. It was a virus transmitted by bats and killing hundreds of people across the globe.

We both thought, "Dang. Oh how sad. As if we didn't have enough problems of our own already."

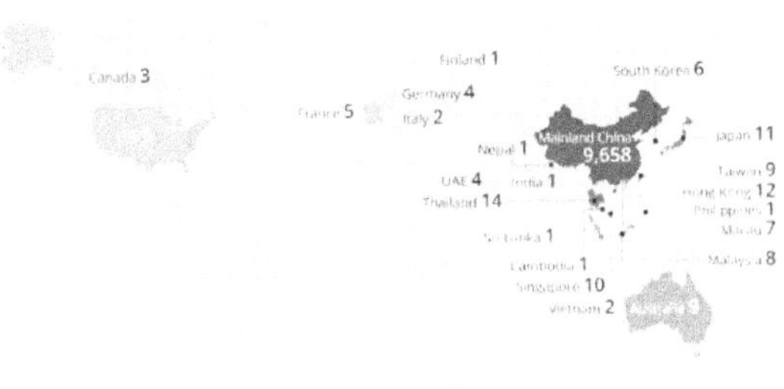

CORONAVIRUS MAP

So I turned the channel to HBO and we enjoyed a good movie instead.

The next few days was spent in bed recuperating and trying to make sense of the imbalance that my body felt. I continued to have shortness of breath and thanks to my friend Tony I was reminded to read the side effects of my new medication. And sure enough the side effects of Brilinta's included 'shortness of breath'.

We used the next two weeks to contemplate how much our life will change post heart attack. We mostly talked about the commitment and strength of our love. It was also about our dreams of the future.

RED ROCK CANYON

As we drove within view of the Red Rock Canyon I heard Alline speak under her breath, "There you are. You mountains almost took away my baby's life."

I realized that I needed to be more aware of the fact that my condition had a profound effect on Alline. Sometimes when an individual is going through a difficult period there is a tendency to think that life is all about them. It is not. Life altering events should always be connected to the 'we'. So we agreed not to ever take life for granted and live each day in the moment.

KEITH SWEAT

In early January I had purchased tickets to see a Keith Sweat concert at the Buffalo Bill Casino in Primm, Nevada. It was a Valentine's Day suprise for Alline. I was not going to allow the last minute turn of events to prevent us from celebrating our love. So on February 15, 2020 we drove to Primm and enjoyed a wonderful concert. Keith Sweat was off the chain and we sang along on every song! We lived in the moment.

On February 25th, two days after my 65th birthday, it was time for my 2nd heart procedure. Doctor Uma was confident that I would spend a minimum amount of time in the hospital. 15 minutes after checking into hospital admissions a nurse called my name. It was time for my final procedure.

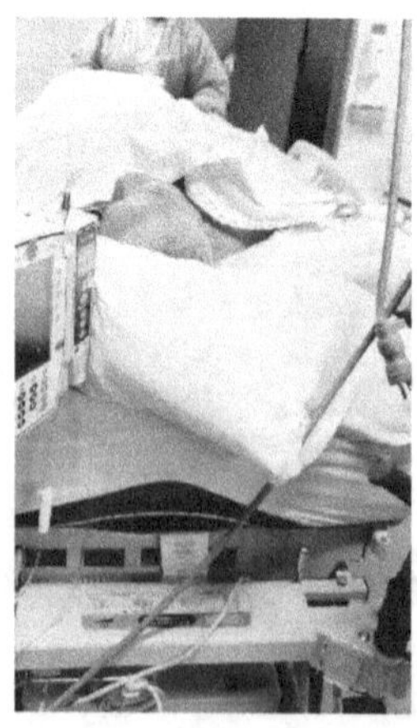

I was given a space in pre-op where I changed into my gown and laid in a bed with Alline close by.

Doctor Uma appeared as I was being rolled into the operating room. We waved and he asked, "Are you ready?"

I responded, "Let's get it done."

Three nurses were waiting for me as I arrived. It was the same room as before but a different crew from my first surgery. Two females and one male. So I made sure to inform them about the writing of a book. Then I checked the clock on the wall for the start time.

The nurse whose job it was to prep the actual entry area was surprised when I told her that I had already shaved my groin area to give her a 'head start'.

She laughed, "Well good for you. Too bad we're not going through the groin. This time we're going through your wrist. But thank you anyway since I have to prep the groin just in case we have a problem with the wrist."

I was shocked that Doctor Uma was going through the vein in my wrist to apply the stent. I had never heard of such a thing.

There was a lot of chatter and laughter between the nurses as they continued to prep me for surgery.

The head nurse walked in and examined my wrist. She asked who prepped the wrist area because it was done incorrectly. When no one volunteered she stated rather flatly, "I am not joking. You all better get your act together."

The operating room fell quiet as the team switched from the frat house party atmosphere to complete professionalism. There was obvious respect for the head nurse and her expectations.

I thought, "Yes! This is going in my book."

The nurse asked if I was okay and just like during the first surgery I answered, "Just waiting on you to get started." Then I looked up at clock and noticed that I had lost 30 minutes. Smiling, the nurse informed me that the procedure was already done, everything went well, and Doctor Uma was in the waiting room talking with my wife.

It was music to my ears to hear the words 'everything went well' and I couldn't help but hear Bill Withers in my head singing, *"And something without warning ... Bears heavy on my mind ... And the world's alright with me ... And I know it's gonna be A lovely day ...".*
As I was wheeled out of the operating room Alline came into view. And Bill kept singing, *"Then I look at you and the world's alright with me. Just one look at you and I know it's gonna be A lovely day. When the day that lies ahead of me Seems impossible to face ... Then I look at you And the world's alright with me ...".*

We were moved into the recovery area where I would be monitored for 4 hours before being released to go home.

Alline used this time to bring me up to speed on my condition. Explaining that according to Doctor Uma everything went well. To show her appreciation she had reached out to shake his hand but instead he gave her a huge hug ... bringing Alline to a place of what felt like a sense of confidence that everything was going to be okay.

This time, upon release by the hospital, I walked out of the recovery room and to the car on my own two feet. It was difficult to tell if Alline was pissed or impressed when I hopped into the car. From the drivers side she turned towards me and with a glare asked how I felt. I could see both the glower and felicity in her eyes as they danced over my face with care.

In this space is where I am drawn into her orbit. Where she has an absolutely irresistible way of making you feel her love. And so you can't help but reciprocate by loving her back more.

I simply smiled and said, "Living the dream."

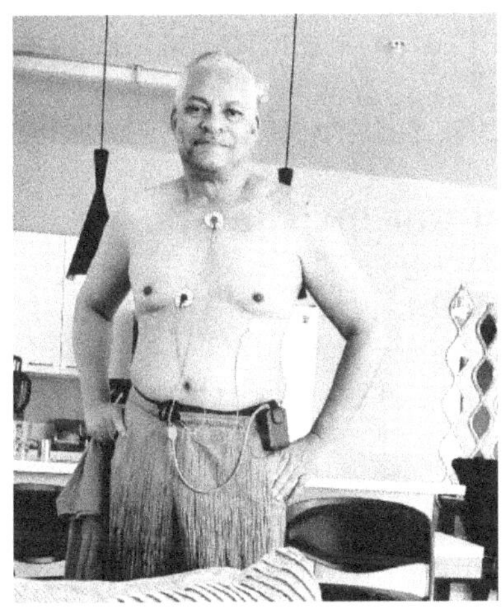

HEART MONITOR

For the next few days I had to wear a heart monitor and complete four ultrasounds. While waiting 2 more weeks to see Doctor Uma for the test results I was struck by sadness.

The news spoke of the coronavirus everyday as more and more people were getting infected. The death rate was skyrocketing in Italy and for older people across the globe with underlying heart or lung disease.

Alline and I both worked in an environment ripe for the covid-19 spread. A place where people from all over the world traveled.

The Luxor Hotel and Casino called us on multiple occasions to work during the outbreak. We became concerned about our own safety and started turning down the shifts offered. Shortly thereafter MGM closed all their properties on the Las Vegas strip until further notice. Then the Nevada governor issued quarantine guidelines for everyone living in the state.

The tightening chest pain along with the shortness of breath continued to be disturbing. The chest pain would come and go with no rhyme or reason. I refused to speak on it at nauseous because I didn't want Alline to worry. Though occassionally I would mention it just enough so if it became a problem she would be aware.

I pondered my decision to supress how I was truly feeling and it became clear that old habits were hard to break.

So while laying in bed during the government lockdown I decided to keep with our promise to live in the moment and expressed to Alline my deepest concerns about the pain in my chest.

Alline laid next to me with her head on my chest and explained to me that everything was going to work out fine because she felt safe, secure, special, and satisfied. God hadn't brought me down from the mountains to watch me die. I felt as if she must have heard something from inside the cavity of my chest because I could feel her body and her mind give way to a higher power.

As I closed my eyes to sleep my mind could hear Weekend Players singing about my Angel, *"Like a feather falling My hearts calling you Angel ... My desert heart's in bloom. Don't take away too soon 'Cause I found me an Angel. Gave wings to my heart. Love has found me an Angel. My devotion is true...".*

Waking the next morning was the moment that my heartbeat felt authentic. Only the shortness of breath existed. The dull pain in my chest had metamorphosed into a beat of strength and confidence.

It was time to go see Doctor Uma. We were ushered into a room where our temperature was taken by a nurse to insure that we didn't have the coronavirus.

Shortly thereafter Doctor Uma walked into the exam room and stood in front of me saying, "Now you know that you had a significant heart attack?" Then he stepped back to get a good look at me, "How are you feeling?"

I answered, "Well I was feeling great until about 30 seconds ago."

Alline and I laughed uneasily as we both understood the significance of the word 'significant'.

While smiling and nodding his head in appreciation of my humor Doctor Uma spoke, "So I have all four of your ultrasound results. The chest, legs, heart, and neck checking for possible damage and blockage. All four results came back 100%. It is as if nothing happened. Usually we expect some damage with such a signif... heart attack. Even my nurse was shocked that there was absolutely no damage to the heart.

Alline asked, "Nothing?"

I asked,"What about the heart monitor?"

Doctor Uma spoke, "Nothing of consequence. There was an occasional blip but that's normal."

With a look of quizzical amazement Alline asked again except this time it sounded more like a statement, "Nothing."

Doctor Uma, "No. Everything looks good."

Suppressing the sound of music that was trying to consume my mind I asked,"You're saying that I can resume 100% of all my activities in life? Hiking, having sex, and drinking wine but not necessarily in that order?"

With a shy smile Doctor Uma stated, "Yes. You are no longer 'at risk' and can do whatever you like."

Alline spoke again, "We have a list of things to ask."

We reviewed our now insignificant list of concerns. With the exception of switching from Brilinta to a generic blood thinner to prevent shortness of breath there was nothing else to say or do.

I took out my cell phone and showed Doctor Uma a mock up bookcover of my upcoming book 'Heart Attack at Red Rock Canyon' to be released in July 2020. And I told him not to worry though because I'll be kind to him. He suggested that after I get the book published we go and celebrate with a glass of wine. There was laughter all the way round.

In as much as we wanted to hug Doctor Uma we couldn't because of the coronavirus. So we just thanked him profusely for saving my life. And thanked the entire staff for their support.

The drive home was surreal. We understood that words matter and Doctor Uma's use of the word 'significant' meant that I was blessed to be still living on this earth. Most of the drive was spent in silence as we, each within our own thoughts, came to terms with mortality.

We had lived the previous two months under an umbrella of fear and uncertainty. And I had mentally prepared myself for more bad news. But instead, we were just told by Doctor Uma that life was normal again. I almost felt disappointed that my heart and health was excellent. But today was a day for rejoicing even with the coronavirus hanging over our heads.

We walked into our home and Alline went straight to the bedroom and I heard the bathroom door close. The bathroom door opened as I entered the bedroom and there she stood stark naked. We had gotten our life back and it was time for celebration.

As Alline and I held each other in bed that night I felt guilty because all I could think about was the fact that I got back the opportunity to climb Gunsight Notch. My life would feel incomplete without going back to successfully climb the mountain that changed my life. The third time around should be a charm. My only concern was convincing Alline to approve my plan because I had already committed to never climbing another peak.

With Alline's head laying on my chest I could feel the ambience of happiness exhibited in her body language. It was as if the world had been lifted from her shoulders. This day had marked a new beginning in our life. And as my eyes closed I could feel the need for 'Sleep' as Amanaska spoke, *"Deep in the night when I hear no sound I feel my heartbeat slowing down. My mind's released and free to wander As I sleep ... We feel lost and we feel found When we sleep ... Two worlds colliding in my head. I watch you as you sleep...".*

I could smell the fresh scent of wild cherry in Alline's hair as I fell asleep.

Things began to change fast. As a country the coronavirus began to consume our lives. The governor of Nevada called for a complete quarantine of the state and all the hospitality businesses on the Las Vegas Strip was shuttered. Uncertainty flooded the entire world as the death toll continued to rise. Over 50,000 human souls were lost in the United States alone.

I was given a clean bill of health and the quarantine gave Alline and I an opportunity to do some making up. To make up for the days we didn't say I love you. To make up for the days we should've gone but we didn't go. To make up for the days we missed sharing our feelings of love. To make up for the days we should've laughed without reason. And for all the days we should've been together if only we had known each other.

We decided to make this the best adventure a pandemic has ever seen by travelling to every beautiful destination within a 3 hour drive from our home base. And we did ...

LOVELL CANYON

WILLOW BEACH

COLORADO RIVER SOUTH COVE

NELSON'S LANDING

KATHERINE'S LANDING

PRINCESS COVE

FIVE MILE LANDING

GUANO POINT

EAGLE POINT

We made the rounds choosing a different destination

every week. From Lovell Canyon to Katherine's Landing,

to Nelson's Landing, to South Cove, to Temple Bar, to Lake

Mohave, to Willow Beach, to Needles, and to the beautiful

Grand Canyon West. We enjoyed the solitude and

sanctuary that we discovered near the Colorado River.

Pure unbridled happiness ...

Then the entire world witnessed the death of George Floyd by 4 police officers on national television.

Pure unbridled murder ...

Once again my heart was attacked ...

I could not stop a 'Return To Innocence' as I listened to the call of the Elders Drinking Song while Enigma played in my mind, "Love, devotion, feeling, emotion. Don't be afraid to be weak. Don't be too proud to be strong. Just look into your heart. That will be the return to yourself. The return to innocence ...".

I began to cry as the traditional Amis chant of Chinese descendants tugged at my heart. I was gripped with pain. Except it was not a dull chest pain. Something else was aching in my soul and I wasn't sure why.

Enigma continued, "If you want, then start to laugh. If you must, then start to cry. Be yourself, don't hide. Just believe in destiny. Don't care what people say. Just follow your own way. Don't give up and use the chance. To return to innocence."

I have always followed my own heart. And I have always chosen the road less traveled. And I have always believed in destiny. And I have always dreamed of a life full of adventure, happiness, and peace.

But times did exist where I had almost given up. Times when I felt that my death would be more valuable than my life. And everytime I was faced with the choice, I chose life.

George Floyd was not given a choice. His murder by the hands of rouge cops released an anger inside my soul that had remained dormant because it was too painful to let bubble to the surface of my being. During my lifetime search for everlasting peace I had learned to supress those feelings that could lead me to a place of violence.

But there was something gnawing at my thoughts that was creating a hurt in my heart. Then I realized that I was just now truly coming to terms with the enigma of racism that permeated my soul...

Thinking about Colin Kaepernick and how he was

whiteballed. Thinking about how I refuse to watch another football game until he is reinstated.

Thinking about Tupac Shakur and how he was gunned down in the streets. Thinking about how I believed his death was premeditated by the powers that be.

Thinking about Muhammad Ali and how he was whiteballed from boxing. Thinking about how I would never watch another boxing match until he was allowed to fight again.

Thinking about Nelson Mandela and how he survived 27 years of unjust incarceration. Thinking about how I swore to never buy another diamond until he was freed.

Thinking about Robert Kennedy and how he was assassinated. Thinking about how racism was a hate that knew no bounds.

Thinking about Dr. Martin Luther king Jr. and how he was assassinated. Thinking about how I would never turn the other cheek again.

Thinking about Malcolm X and his assassination. Thinking about how I would never trust the government again.

Thinking about the Vietnam War and how we lost untold black soldiers. Thinking about how to never fight any white man's war.

Thinking about how they all always had a knee on their neck.

Thinking about those times when my father told me stories of not being allowed to become a fighter pilot because of discrimination.

Thinking about his military evaluation as a good negro boy.

Thinking about his experiences with racism as a Pension Trust Examiner for the IRS.

Thinking about him being kicked out the offices of prominent companies and having to return with Federal Agents.

Thinking about how C.E.O.s would turn beak red and call him nigger.

Thinking about how someone always had their knee on his neck.

Shackles were being passed from one generation to the next as I began thinking about my own pain of racism endured at every step and stage of life. Someone always with their knee on my neck.

Thinking about how the toxic environment for a black man in white corporate america prevented me from being my best self.

Thinking about how I would be the only minority executive in the company.

Thinking about the times I was called a token.

Thinking about how the guniune me had to remain hidden over 8 hours a day 6 days a week for almost 30 years.

Thinking about how I had spent a lifetime trying to please the master of my ancestors.

Thinking about how good it felt to please them so that I could receive a monetary raise or get an award for my achievements.

Thinking about the time I discovered that I was the

lowest paid general manager making the most profit and running the highest volume.

Thinking about how hurtful it was when master refused to acknowledge my successes in front of peers.

Thinking about those peers who were obviously less qualified got promoted beyond my rank.

Thinking about how these things only made me work harder and smarter because being equal meant being twice as good.

Thinking about how much I wanted to receive the desired praise from my masters.

Thinking about those times when I blew the whistle on inequality in the workplace and was whiteballed.

Thinking about those times when my bosses were fired for discrimination and it meant a c.l.d.(career limiting decision) for me.

Thinking about having bosses make promises to me only to break it weeks later.

Thinking about all the good white executives I worked with along the way that were complicit.

Thinking about how I had to pick and choose carefully my battles of witnessed discrimination.

All the years of hidden pain attacked my heart in the flash of seconds. The inescapable truth of my existence was laid to bare on the ground beneath the knee. I was experiencing a different sort of heart attack. It was a hurt more devastating than the heart attack at Red Rock Canyon. And I couldn't breathe.

'In and out. In and out. In and out.'

The anger excelled as I thought of all the white peers who befriended me only to use that friendship to seek damning information and promote themselves.

Thinking of the times when my salary was less than, yet my job was more than.
Thinking about the times I was refused employment for being 'overqualified'.
Thinking of the moments when my bosses lied to their

bosses in my presence and I ended up taking the fall.

Thinking about how I traveled through the small towns of the south to train and develop white managers.

Thinking about how I had to leave before nightfall or risk being physically attacked.

Thinking about how living in those small towns made me hear the word nigger more often than I could have ever imagined.

Thinking about how my heart raced uncontrollably for no apparent reason every time a cop pulled me over.

Thinking about the time my boss said that the south should have won the civil war.

Thinking about the times I had to undercover advise people of color on how to manipulate white executives to achieve success.

Thinking about how racist executives raised their ugly heads in corporate meetings and I said nothing because I wanted to be considered for the next promotion.

Thinking about how I was used to support the unspoken

rule of always hiring and maintaining a majority white staff even in predominantly black areas.

Thinking about how 'read between the lines' jokes and deniability jokes were told in my presence as if I was too dense to understand the racist connotation.

Thinking about how I swore to eliminate from my being the desire to seek their approval only to find myself once again seeking approval.

Thinking about the multiple corporate diversity training programs and how white managers scoffed at the implication.

Thinking about how many genuine white friendships were left at the table for fear of betrayal.

Thinking about the thousands of people that I managed and cared about but abandoned because I gave up and looked for greener pastures.

Thinking about how greener pastures simply didn't exist.

Thinking about how racism stole my dream of liberty and justice for all.

Thinking about how my desire to please morphed into

anger. Thinking about how my anger manifested into corruption. Thinking about how eventually my corruption created a manipulative person immune to caring anymore about achieving success in white america.

Thinking about how I allowed them to adversely affect my character and principles. Only to discover that character and principle is of my own choosing.

Thinking about how I was driven to hate myself and wanted to commit suicide.

Thinking about how God intervened and stopped my craving for the white man's pat on my back.

Thinking about how at peace I felt 15 years ago on the day I stepped away from it all so that I could actually be the man I dreamed to be.

As quickly as each of these thoughts raced into my heart they were. released into the universe. Faith allowed me to understand that God was freeing me from the past and blessing me with adventures to come. The pain I was feeling melted away in tears of happiness.

Yet, I felt such sadness that this all started with Kobe Bryant's death, then the coronavirus killing thousands, and ending with George Floyd's murder. I wondered if they all had to lose their lives in order to save mine and millions of other people across the world. I had to believe that it is all part of a master plan that will continue to create seismic shifts in our humanity to form a more perfect union.

The world had been witness to the murder of a man in the hands of our protectors. Mankind shifted at the horror of it all and change began taking place around the globe. God had taken Kobe from me at Gunsight Notch and George in front of my television eyes so that they could save my soul.

And though we all have our own individual stories the coronavirus shows that we are all bound together throughout life until death. It does not discriminate. What can affect one of us can effect all of us. We must have faith that it just travels the world according to Gods plan to save all our souls as we move towards infinity. It reminded me of something that I had heard from somewhere, "If you want a good laugh, tell God your plans."

Following the Elders chant my own Enigma spoke inside my mind, "That's not the beginning of the end. That's the return to yourself. A return to innocence." The Elders Drinking Song was a toast to happiness.

At age 65 I had finally returned to myself. I was finally the complete man I was meant to be. I had finally found my peace.

MY BALCONY

I sat on my balcony overlooking Red Rock Canyon while listening to 'Back To The Rivers Of Belief' by Enigma, "Take a deep breath ... I look inside my heart. I look inside my soul. I promise you I will return."

I dreamed of the day when I would successfully climb to the summit of Gunsight Notch. And I knew my third attempt at reaching the peak of my life's enigma was near.

I felt it in my heart ...

MARC GRIFFIN / GUNSIGHT NOTCH

IN LOVING MEMORY

THANK YOU

Since the writing of ENDLESS DREAMS our lives have been witness to much change.

The touch of death constantly surrounds us yet life continues moving forward towards infinity. Leading us all to our final resting place. Some sooner some later but we all must eventually find our place.

I no longer morn those who have left this world. I celebrate them for God has given them a place in heaven. The loss of my older sister has brought her peace and for that I can only be grateful.

To witness our daughter, Kristin Walker, traverse the unfolding challenges of her life's adventure has been a blessing. She is our legacy.

To all our family and friends hold on to your happiness every single day because life on this earth is too short and is never guaranteed. Love hard.

Alline and Marc

LIVING A LIFE OF ENDLESS DREAMS